CULTURES OF THE WORLD

MEXICO

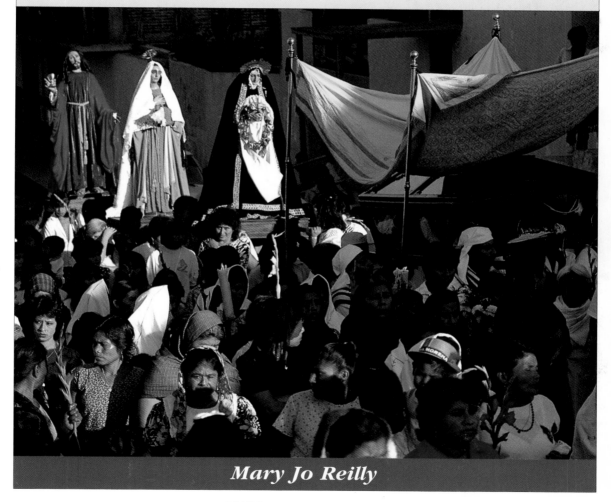

Mary Jo Reilly

MARSHALL CAVENDISH
New York • London • Sydney

Editorial Director	Shirley Hew
Managing Editor	Shova Loh
Editors	Roseline Lum
	Siow Peng Han
	Leonard Lau
	MaryLee Knowlton
Picture Editor	Jane Duff
Production	Edmund Lam
Design	Tuck Loong
	Lee Woon Hong
	Dani Phoa
	Ong Su Ping
	Katherine Tan
Illustrator	Thomas Koh

Reference edition published 1991 by
Marshall Cavendish Corporation
147 West Merrick Road
Freeport, Long Island
N.Y. 11520

Printed in Singapore by
Kim Hup Lee Printing Co. Pte Ltd

Originated and designed by
Times Books International
an imprint of Times Editions Pte Ltd
Times Center, 1 New Industrial Road
Singapore 1953
Telex: 37908 EDTIME Fax: 2854871

Library of Congress Cataloging-in-Publication Data:
  Reilly, Mary-Jo, 1964–
  Mexico / by Mary-Jo Reilly.
    p. cm.—(Cultures Of The World)
  Includes bibliographical references and index.
  Summary: Introduces the geography, history,
    culture, and lifestyles of Mexico.
  ISBN 1-85435-385-3:
    1. Mexico. [1. Mexico.] I. Title. II. Series.
F1208.5.R45 1991
972—dc20   90-22469
                                  CIP
                                  AC

INTRODUCTION

Although Mexico shares the North American continent with the United States and Canada, its heritage belongs more to Latin America. Indeed, Mexico serves as a geographical and cultural bridge between North and South America, containing elements of both, yet maintaining a strong identity of its own. Mexico is at once the most ancient and the most modern country in Latin America.

As Spain's wealthiest colony in the Americas, Mexico has an architectural richness comparable to Europe's. As a land of great Indian civilizations, it offers ruins as fascinating as those in Greece. As a modern nation, its unique culture, blending Indian and Spanish music, dance, cuisine, handicrafts and arts, is unparalleled.

Mexico's importance in the world will only continue to grow. In this book, one of the series, *Cultures of the World*, we will examine Mexico's exciting past, its turbulent present and its vibrant future.

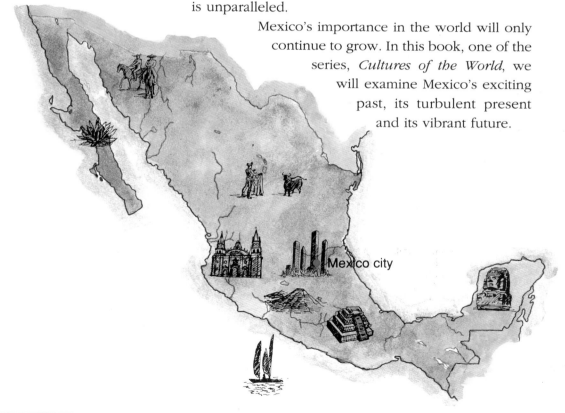

Mexico city

CONTENTS

Outside the modern cities of Mexico, life flows by at a more leisurely and relaxed pace.

3 INTRODUCTION

7 GEOGRAPHY
Land regions • Climate • Flora • Fauna

17 HISTORY
The Mayans • The Aztecs • Spanish Conquest • The colonial period • Independence • Benito Juárez and the Reform Period • The Porfiriato • Revolution and aftermath

29 GOVERNMENT
The three branches • The army • The PRI • Mexican-American relations

35 ECONOMY
Sources of revenue

45 MEXICANS
The earliest settlers • The Indians • Mestizos • Population problems • Costume

53 LIFESTYLE
Family: the core of society • Rites of passage • Machismo • Women • Customs • Social conditions • Casa Mexicana

69 RELIGION
Anti-church reforms • The Church today

CONTENTS

75 LANGUAGE

Indian languages • Hey amigo!

83 THE ARTS

Pre-Columbian art and architecture • The art scene today • Crafts and folk arts • Music • Dance • Modern architecture • Literature

97 LEISURE

The bullfight • Other sports • The charros

105 FESTIVALS

Independence day • The day of the dead • Feast of our Lady of Guadalupe • The Christmas season

115 FOOD

Staples: corn to tortillas • Traditional meals • Traditional drinks • Markets and food stalls • Mealtimes

124 MAP OF MEXICO

126 QUICK NOTES

127 GLOSSARY AND BIBLIOGRAPHY

128 INDEX

The folk crafts of Mexico reflect its unique Indian heritage.

GEOGRAPHY

MEXICO IS THE NORTHERNMOST country of Latin America. It is a horn-shaped country bounded by the United States on the north, the Gulf of Mexico and the Caribbean Sea on the east, Guatemala and Belize on the southeast, and the Pacific Ocean on the south and west.

Brazil and Argentina are the only Latin American countries larger than Mexico in area, and only Brazil has a larger population.

Mexico's early civilizations were quite different from its current borders. To the south, it reached into Guatemala, Belize, El Salvador and parts of Honduras. In the north, it spread about 300 miles further north from the Central Valley of Mexico City. This historical area is referred to as Mesoamerica.

Above: **The geographical regions of Mexico.**

Opposite: **Mt.Popocatépetl is one of the largest volcanoes in Mexico. The Aztecs once worshiped the volcano as a god.**

LAND REGIONS

Most of Mexico is made up of mountains and plateaus. Two great mountain chains, the Sierra Madre Oriental and the Sierra Madre Occidental, run north-south across the country. These two chains are part of the Andes range that begins in South America. When the range hits Mexico, it splits into two. The western, or occidental, range then continues northward into the United States, linking up with the Rocky Mountains.

Few countries have a more diverse landscape and climate than Mexico. Within short distances of each other are snow-capped mountains, resort beaches, plateaus, barren deserts, rich farmland and tropical rainforests. Mexico can be divided into five general regions based on landforms, climate and vegetation patterns.

Desert of Baja California.

THE PACIFIC NORTHWEST This region covers the states of Baja California Norte, Baja California Sur, the western part of Sonora, Sinaloa and northern Nayarit. It is very dry, and Baja California, an 800-mile-long peninsula, is basically a desert.

The landscape of the Pacific Northwest is dominated by desert brush and many cacti and agave species, as there is little rainfall. There are pockets of land where farming occurs, but the land is difficult to cultivate.

The Colorado River delta forms a large lowland in the northeastern part of this region. As the delta grew, it cut off and dried up the northernmost and southernmost parts of the Gulf of California, forming the Imperial Valley in California, and the Mexicali Valley in Mexico.

The Pacific Northwest's mainland coastal strip is better for farming because it has fertile valleys that are irrigated by rivers, including the Colorado, Yaqui and Fuerte. In addition to farmland, these basins support cattle ranches, and rich copper and silver mines.

VOLCANOES

Most of the mountains in Mexico have volcanic origins. Some are still active. One of the largest, Popocatépetl, which means "smoking mountain" in the Nahuatl Indian language, has not erupted since 1702. From time to time though, it still releases huge, billowing clouds of smoke. The Aztecs considered Popocatépetl and the smaller volcano next to it, Ixtaccihuatl, or "sleeping woman," to be gods.

The youngest volcano in Mexico was "born" on February 7,1943. Called Paricutín, it emerged from the middle of a cornfield. It grew to 1,700 feet, poured out a billion tons of lava and destroyed several villages. It ceased activity in 1952, although it has the potential to become active again in the future. The most recent volcanic activity in Mexico occurred in 1982 in the state of Chiapas, when the volcano Chinchon exploded, killing many people.

THE CENTRAL PLATEAU It is located between the two Sierra Madre mountain chains. While irrigation is needed in the arid northern part, the southern areas contain some of the richest, most fertile farmland in all of Mexico. Summer rains usually provide good enough growing conditions for small grains. The western part of the plateau also contains the manufacturing centers of Guadalajara, León, Querétaro and San Luis Potosí.

The castor oil plant. Cash crops are grown in this most fertile region of Mexico.

Above top: **Farming in the Yucatán Peninsula.**

Above bottom: **One of the huge sacred wells of the Mayans.**

THE GULF COASTAL PLAIN AND THE YUCATAN

The geographies of the Gulf Coastal Plain and the Yucatán Peninsula change gradually as they go from north to south.

They start out dry in the north and get wetter and wetter until they turn into tropical rainforests in the south. The Gulf Coastal Plain is primarily located in the states of Nuevo León, Tamaulipas, Veracruz and Tabasco.

Farming is possible in the northern part of the Gulf Coastal Plain, which is near rivers. The Yucatán Peninsula has no rivers. It is basically a limestone plateau with underground channels to the sea.

Huge pits have formed where the roofs of these channels have fallen in. These pits were once the sacred wells of the Mayan Indians.

THE SIERRA VOLCANICA TRANSVERSAL It forms a major geological break with the Central Plateau. Hundreds of volcanic mountains, countless cinder cones, lava flows, ash deposits, hot springs and other amazing landmarks tell of past and present volcanic activity.

The soil and climate of this region have made it very attractive for human settlement. It is the most populated area of Mexico. Mexico City, Toluca and Puebla are located here. Unfortunately, the basins located in the transversal trap the dirty air generated by the cities, making air pollution a major problem.

THE SOUTHERN UPLANDS This region is characterized by steep mountain ridges and deep gorges cut by mountain streams. Several of Mexico's most popular tourist destinations are in this region, including the famed resort city of Acapulco, and Monte Albán, the ancient Indian religious center.

The ancient city of Monte Albán lies within the hilly regions of the Southern Uplands.

The highest peaks in Mexico are always covered with snow. Frost, while not common, is possible above 6,000 feet.

CLIMATE

Most people think of Mexico as a hot, dry country, but this is really a misconception. The Tropic of Cancer cuts Mexico almost exactly in half, putting the southern part of the country in the tropical zone and the northern part in the temperate zone.

However, in Mexico the climate is determined as much by altitude as by latitude. Thus the so-called tropical zone, which includes a wide variety of altitudes, actually has hot, temperate and cool areas. And the temperate zone has some of the driest deserts to be found anywhere.

Generally, the coastal lowlands are hot, the plateaus are temperate and the mountains are cool. Mexicans define these three temperature zones as *tierra caliente* (hot land, up to 3,000 feet), *tierra templada* (temperate land, 3,000–6,000 feet) and *tierra fria* (cold land, above 6,000 feet).

The northern Yucatán Peninsula is very dry while the southeastern part of the peninsula, where the tropical rain forests are located, is extremely humid.

Mexico City, which lies about 7,000 feet above sea level, is warm during the day and cool at night. The north and northwest, which belong to the desert belt of the Northern Hemisphere, are very dry and consist largely of deserts and semi-deserts.

Rain falls mostly in the mountains near the coasts, making the interior of Mexico very dry. Generally, the east coast receives much more rain than the Pacific coast.

Only about 12% of the country gets enough rainfall for growing good crops without irrigation, and almost half the country receives less than 24 inches of rain annually. Except in Baja California, most of the rain falls between summer and early autumn.

As temperature changes throughout the year are only moderate, Mexico has virtually no seasons.

Cactus plants can be found in many parts of Mexico as the climate is generally hot and dry.

The wetter regions of Mexico have lush tropical forests.

FLORA

The enormous differences in climate naturally result in an enormous variety of plant life in Mexico. The arid northern, northwestern and central regions produce plants which are adapted to a limited water supply, such as cactus, agave, cassava, mesquite and brush plants.

In the south, east and on the western coasts, tropical vegetation such as rainforests, savannah vegetation, grazing land and spiny plants dominate. Some of Mexico's mountains are snow-capped, some are forested and others are barren.

Mexico is also home to what is said to be the oldest living thing on the American continents—a giant ahuete tree which the natives call "El Arbol del Tule"—the Tree of Tula.

The poinsettia, the popular floral symbol of Christmas, is native to Mexico. It is usually found in moist, wet, wooded ravines and rocky hillsides.

FAUNA

In addition to a varied plant life, Mexico has a rich mix of animal life that includes species from both North and South America.

Birds, reptiles, insects and a variety of mammals—including wild sheep, deer, bears, rodents and opossums—are plentiful. The tropical rainforests contain such exotic animals as monkeys, jaguars, wild boars and cougars.

Marine life off the coast of Mexico is equally varied, containing a wealth of fish and marine life. The northernmost stretch

Colorful bright orange monarch butterflies.

of the Pacific coast is washed by the Gulf of California, a sheltered sea that opens to the south into the Pacific Ocean.

The meeting of the distinct marine environments of the Gulf and the Pacific yields a wide variety of fish. Marlin, black sea bass and sailfish, among others, are caught far offshore, while smaller species such as porgy and amberjack are in ample supply closer to the beach.

Perhaps the most spectacular of the mammals off Mexico is the grey whale, which migrates every winter to the waters off Baja California to mate and calve. While almost extinct 50 years ago, the grey whales have made an amazing comeback. At their favorite breeding ground, the number of whales has risen from 250 in 1937 to 18,000 today.

Another previously endangered mammal that has made a remarkable comeback since the beginning of this century is the elephant seal, which is found near Guadalupe Island.

HISTORY

THE FIRST SETTLERS IN MEXICO were nomadic hunter-gatherers from Asia who crossed the Bering Strait in search of meat. Traveling in small groups, they slowly moved south and eventually reached Mexico. Some tribes went on as far south as Chile, but those who stayed behind began to create Mexico's earliest civilizations.

The Olmec developed the first highly civilized culture in Mesoamerica around 1500 B.C. They transmitted their culture to other tribes through trade and war. Today, the Olmec culture is thought to be the origin of many of the later Indian empires.

Opposite and above: **The now silent and empty cities of the Mayans are lasting monuments to a great civilization.**

The Olmec Indians were a tightly organized, very efficient group ruled by religious and civilian leaders. They built religious centers on the Gulf Coast, in what is today southern Veracruz and Tabasco, and established colonies in central and southern Mexico.

The most enduring legacy of the Olmec Indians is their art, especially their stone sculptures. Some of these sculptures are heads with both Asian and African features. The African features remain a mystery, but they suggest the Olmec population may have had two races. The damaged remains of many of these monuments and sculptures suggest the Olmec civilization came to a violent end around 400 B.C.

For the next 1,700 years many cultures developed, flourished and then faded. Some of the more advanced of these were the Zapotecs and the Mixtecs in southwestern Mexico and at Monte Albán; the Tarascans of Michoacán; and the Totonac of Veracruz, who built the famous Pyramid of the Niches in Tajín.

The Mayans were a highly artistic people who built beautiful cities and sculptures.

THE MAYANS

Perhaps the most spectacular of all American Indian cultures is the Mayan. It was the only ancient culture in the Americas to develop an original system of writing, which it used to record chronology, astronomy, history and religion. Their system of mathematics was an achievement not equaled for centuries in Europe. The 365-day Mayan year was improved upon only this century. Sculpture, used in architecture, was unequaled both in terms of beauty and dignity.

Before the Mayan civilization reached its peak (about A.D. 200–800) the cities of Palenque and Tikal were the centers of a civilization that numbered close to 14 million people. The Mayan culture declined around A.D. 900. Nobody really knows why, but experts suspect that the Mayans were hit by natural disasters as well as invasions from hostile tribes.

THE AZTECS

The Aztecs rose more quickly and became more powerful than any other group in the history of Mexico. Before their rise, the Aztecs were a poor nomadic tribe living in the valleys of Mexico. But by the time of the Spanish Conquest, the Aztec empire included most of Mesoamerica.

About 1325, the Aztecs arrived on Lake Texcoco near present-day Mexico City. They saw, on an island in the middle of the lake, an eagle perched on a cactus holding a serpent in its mouth, and they interpreted it as a sign from the gods to settle there. They constructed a city called Tenochtitlán. Today the eagle with the serpent in its mouth is the symbol of Mexico. It appears on flags, currency and government seals.

The first houses in Tenochtitlán were built on rafts in the middle of the shallow lake. One hundred years later, Tenochtitlán became an elegant, sophisticated city and the Aztecs became a sophisticated tribe of fierce warriors. Although the Aztec society was dominated by the nobles, priests, military and merchant classes, it made provisions for the common man as well. For example, the educational system was more advanced than in any other Mesoamerican civilization.

The Aztecs were an aggressive, violent people dominated by their military and their god of war. The army led many successful wars of conquest, and soldiers were rewarded with land grants and positions of wealth and influence. Prisoners were used for slaves and sacrifices, which the Aztecs believed were necessary to please their gods. Methods of human sacrifice included execution, drowning, whipping and tearing hearts out while they were still beating. But the Aztec pride and cruelty would eventually play a role in their downfall.

Above: **Everyday life in the Aztec city of Tenoch-titlán. (Mural by Diego Rivera)**

Below: **These religious carvings depict the heads of the Aztec rain god and Quetzalcóatl.**

19

TEOTIHUACAN

Teotihuacán is the largest, most impressive and most well known of all ancient Mexican religious centers. Built around 300 B.C. by Indians of unknown origin, it dominated the area until its mysterious decline and fall around A.D. 700. At its peak, Teotihuacán's population was over 100,000.

Teotihuacán is laid out in a grid and dominated by the Pyramid of the Sun. Other significant buildings in the city included the Pyramid of the Moon and the Temple of Quetzalcóatl.

The people of Teotihuacán were highly skilled artists. Their designs suggest their lives revolved around a complex religious system based on the worship of the sun god, the moon goddess, the rain god and the god Quetzalcóatl, which means "feathered serpent."

SPANISH CONQUEST

In 1519, Hernán Cortés and about 500 Spanish adventurers set sail for the
New World of the Americas in search of treasures. Their arrival stunned
the Aztecs, who had never seen ships, horses or white people before.

When word reached the Aztec emperor Moctezuma, the highly religious
and deeply reflective leader thought Cortés must be the god Quetzalcóatl,
whom legend said would return to Tenochtitlán that same year. To
appease this "god," and to get him to leave, Moctezuma sent Cortés gold,
silver and other riches. When Cortés saw this treasure, he became
determined to conquer the Aztecs and have the wealth all for himself.

Had Moctezuma fought Cortés right away, it is unlikely the Spaniards
would have survived as they were vastly outnumbered by the millions of
Indians. But because Moctezuma waited, and because Cortés had the
good fortune of finding a translator who could communicate with the
Indians, the Spanish leader was able to form alliances with the Aztec's
enemies. These reinforcements, together with the Spaniards' sophisticated
weapons, were too much for Moctezuma's people. Though they fought
bitterly and bravely, the Aztecs were soon conquered.

The Monastery of San Agustín. The Spanish Conquest soon brought many Catholic missionaries to Mexico.

THE COLONIAL PERIOD

Once the Spanish had conquered Mexico, they were faced with the enormous job of governing it—not an easy task, given the new colony's vast size, huge population and enormous distance from Spain. The Spanish government began by issuing decrees that regulated nearly every aspect of the new colony's lifestyle. However, of far more importance than these decrees to the lives of the Indians was the arrival of the Catholic Church.

Dedicated Catholic friars traveled throughout Mexico in their quest to reform and educate the masses. Unfortunately, as they spread, so did the European diseases they brought with them, diseases for which the Indians had no immunity.

And despite the Church's initial idealism, economic demands created practices that abused, neglected and enslaved the Indians. The combination of Spanish diseases and Spanish abuses caused a huge number of Indian deaths. In one of the most catastrophic population declines in history, the Indian population fell from about 25 million in 1519 to just one million in 1700.

INDEPENDENCE

Although millions of Indians and *mestizos* were abused and suffering because of the inequalities in an extremely class-based society, it was the Creoles—Spaniards born in Mexico, who started the movement for independence from Spain.

Resentful of Spain's interference in Mexico's burgeoning economy, and inspired by ideas of individual rights and freedom from the American and French revolutions, the Creoles began pushing for changes. On September 15, 1810, Father Miguel Hidalgo y Costillo, a 57-year-old parish priest from the town of Dolores, began the rebellion with the now famous *Grito de Dolores*—"cry for independence." The conflict lasted for five years but ultimately failed. In 1820, the fight for independence started again, but this time the Creoles and the *peninsulars*—those born in Spain to white parents, banded together. Their new army met with little resistance, and on September 27, 1821, Agustín de Iturbide was crowned Emperor and head of the new Mexican government. A constitution was written and established in 1823.

The Revolution of 1820. The mural depicts the people and the church uniting in the struggle against Spain. (Mural by Diego Rivera)

But Mexico was not prepared for independence; 300 years of Spanish domination had left it extremely weak and unstable. Emperor Agustín was overthrown after only 11 months. Fifty-six different regimes came and went in the next 40 years. For 30 of those years, Mexico was periodically ruled by dictator-general Antonio Lopez de Santa Anna who lost half of the country's territory to the United States. He was overthrown in 1855 by Benito Juárez, a man who would become one of Mexico's most revered heroes.

BENITO JUAREZ AND THE REFORM PERIOD

Benito Juárez, a pure Zapotec Indian who was orphaned as a young boy and raised by a Franciscan friar, is often called the "Abraham Lincoln of Mexico."

Despite his strict Catholic upbringing, Juárez was instrumental in implementing much-needed reforms to the Catholic Church, and as president of the country (1857–65 and 1867–72), he oversaw the transfer of political power from the Creoles to the *mestizos*.

The Catholic Church in the 19th century was far more wealthy and powerful than the Mexican government, yet it did little to bring about desperately needed political and social changes. In fact, the Church worked against any reforms that would weaken its power.

A statue in tribute to President Benito Juárez.

The conflicts between Church and State eventually escalated into a three-year civil war called the War of the Reform (1858–61). Juárez led the liberals to victory and promptly instituted the reforms.

But in 1864 the Church, helped by France, regained power and exiled Juárez. France established its own emperor, a well-intentioned man named Maximilian. He tried to institute reforms to help the people, but because he was a foreigner, the people did not trust him.

Three years later, with the help of the United States, Juárez was restored to power and the reform laws became a permanent part of the Mexican government. When Juárez died in 1872, Mexico had a constitutional and democratic government.

THE PORFIRIATO

The death of Benito Juárez in 1872 led to another period of instability and ultimately to the dictatorship of Porfirio Díaz. Díaz was a *mestizo* who supported Juárez and his reform movement. But when he ran against Juárez for president and lost, he said the election was fixed and that Juárez shouldn't be allowed to run for president so many times.

Ironically, once Díaz overthrew Juárez's successor in 1876 and took over as head of the government, he ignored his own earlier protests and remained in power for 34 years. His ruthless dictatorship was so significant to Mexican history that the period has its own name: the Porfiriato.

During the Porfiriato, the economy developed enormously but social problems worsened drastically. Many people who supported Díaz became rich, but the majority of the Mexican population lived in poverty.

Porfirio Díaz—President from 1876 to 1911.

By 1910, 100 years after the country's independence, Mexico was a country with great social differences among the people. All the land and wealth were concentrated in the hands of about 20% of the population. The average person had less than before independence.

Díaz was a very shrewd man, but he caused his own downfall by telling a journalist that he was considering retirement. A relatively unknown Mexican named Francisco Madero took Díaz at his word and ran against him for the presidency in 1910.

At first Díaz didn't take his opponent seriously, but Madero's campaign for political reform was so popular and so threatening to Díaz that finally the dictator had him imprisoned until after the election.

Pancho Villa *(opposite)* **and Emiliano Zapata** *(above)* **fought against the rich and the landed ranchers. Once thought of as bandits, today they are revered as national heroes.**

REVOLUTION AND AFTERMATH (1910–40)

Francisco Madero strongly opposed violence, but he saw no other way to overthrow Díaz. So in November 1910, he called for rebellion. Revolutionary bands developed throughout Mexico.

In May 1911, Díaz was forced from office. Madero was subsequently elected president under free and open conditions. He realized economic reforms were necessary, but was unable to implement the changes before being assassinated in a coup in 1913.

After Madero's death, the revolutionary leaders began to quarrel among themselves and with the new president, Venustiano Carranza. Two of these men, Emiliano Zapata and Pancho Villa, believed that reform through politics was practically impossible.

They gathered Indian armies and forcibly took back land they believed rightfully belonged to the Indians. But Zapata and Villa were killed and Carranza eventually prevailed. Today, Villa and Zapata are national heroes.

In 1917, Carranza called a convention to prepare a new constitution. This constitution, still in effect today, laid the groundwork for a new Mexican nation.

It limited presidents to only one term; returned communal land to the peasants; gave the government control over education, the Catholic Church, and farm and oil properties; protected factory workers and generally guaranteed basic democratic freedoms.

Decades of efforts at reform resulted, and in 1934, the peaceful election of Lazaro Cardenas symbolized the success of the revolution. Indeed, the Cardenas presidency, which saw the fulfillment of many of the revolution's ideals, provided the basis for the stability of contemporary Mexico.

GOVERNMENT

MEXICO IS A FEDERAL REPUBLIC divided into 31 states and a federal district. The government is based on the constitution of 1917, which attempts to provide for the goals fought for during the Mexican Revolution and the period that followed, and to create a structure that both eliminates past abuses and prevents further ones.

The constitution divides the government into three branches: executive, legislative and judicial. It also establishes state governments with elected governors and legislatures.

Under the constitution, the federal government has great powers in economic, educational and state matters. The government has used this power to the benefit of the people when it broke up privately-owned farmlands and divided them among the poor, and when it set up a national school system.

Other uses of this power have been more controversial, such as when the government took over a number of industries, including the railroad and petroleum. The federal government also has the authority to suspend a state's constitutional powers, and has done so in the past to settle struggles for leadership.

Although Mexico's government is undergoing great upheaval as it attempts to repair the country's devastated economy and clean up the political system, it has been more stable under the constitution of 1917 than at any other time in its history.

Above: **The President of Mexico—Carlos Salinas de Gotari.**

Opposite: **Inauguration ceremony of President Salinas at the National Palace.**

The National Palace in Mexico City.

THE THREE BRANCHES

The executive branch is headed by a president who is elected to a six-year term. There is no vice-president. If a president does not finish his term, Congress chooses a temporary president to serve until a special or regular election is held. The president may not run for re-election.

The legislative branch is called the Congress. The Congress is divided into two branches: the Senate and the Chamber of Deputies. The Senate has 64 Senators; each is elected to serve a six-year term.

The Chamber of Deputies has 400 members. The Deputies are elected to three-year terms. Members of Congress cannot serve two terms in a row.

The judicial system is headed by the Supreme Court of Justice, followed by 21 circuit courts and 68 district courts. The judges are appointed to serve life terms.

STATE AND LOCAL GOVERNMENT Mexico's 31 states are each headed by a governor. State governors are elected to six-year terms, and may not run for re-election.

The Chamber of Deputies in each state has 9 to 25 members. They, too, are not allowed to serve more than one term in office.

The local government in Mexico is divided into about 2,400 cities or townships called *municipios*. Each is headed by municipal presidents and their respective councils.

THE ARMY

Unlike the armed forces in most other Latin American countries, the Mexican army plays a very insignificant role in the governing of the republic. Realizing the importance of having the army under their control, Mexican presidents have richly rewarded army loyalty and severely punished acts of betrayal.

The unlikelihood that Mexico will get into a war with any of its neighboring countries has allowed Mexican presidents to consistently reduce the army's share of the federal budget.

Mexico has one of the lowest ratios of soldiers to population in Latin America. The army's resulting insignificance has greatly contributed to the stability of the Mexican government. Since 1920, Mexico is the only Latin American country whose government has not experienced a coup attempt.

One of the contributing factors to Mexico's political stability is the non-political role played by the army.

Supporters of the PRI during the election campaign of President Salinas.

THE PRI

The majority political party in Mexico is the *Partido Revolucionario Institucional* (Institutional Revolutionary Party), referred to as the PRI. It was created in 1929 to serve as the official party for the economic and social goals of the Mexican Revolution. It represents almost every major power group in the nation, including labor unions, the business community, financial interests and peasant movements.

For a long time, the other political parties in Mexico have had almost no influence in the national government. Recently, however, this has been changing.

Since its founding, the PRI has won every election for presidency by huge majorities. Although it doesn't take voters for granted, it has been accused of buying votes and fixing elections. Accusations of corruption have led to violent protests.

In the last decade the PRI has experienced several electoral defeats to candidates from the leading opposition party, the *Partido de Accion Nacional* (National Action Party, or PAN). All this has many experts believing that Mexico may no longer be a one-party state.

MEXICAN-AMERICAN RELATIONS

Most Americans don't realize how much the fate of the United States is bound with the fate of Mexico. The truth is, what happens to Mexico greatly affects the United States.

The two countries share a 2,000-mile-long unguarded border. While this fact poses no great threat now, if unrest in Mexico forced the United States to establish border defenses, the cost alone would be devastating.

Over 200,000 Americans owe their jobs to Mexico's continued ability to buy exports from the United States. Mexico is the third largest market in the world for American goods, after Canada and Japan, and its importance in the export market is expected to grow.

Mexican-Americans are the fastest growing political force in the United States. Increasingly, Americans will have to deal with Mexican culture, habits, demands and sensitivities. This is particularly true in cities or states with large Mexican-American populations.

Protest against any U.S. interference in Panama. Events occurring in Latin America are of great concern to both Mexico and the United States.

ECONOMY

FOR MOST OF MEXICO'S HISTORY, the majority of its people have lived off the land. Before the revolution of 1910, most of the land in Mexico was divided into huge estates called *haciendas* that were owned by wealthy landlords. After the revolution, the new government divided most of them into *ejidos,* or communal farms, and distributed them to landless peasants.

The Second World War forced the government to begin producing goods it had been importing. Manufacturing rose in importance while agriculture began to decline. In the 1970s, vast oil reserves were discovered along the eastern coast. Income from oil production fueled the development of manufacturing and service industries. While the price of oil was high, Mexico borrowed money for many construction projects. The government had hoped to create desperately needed jobs and finance broad programs of economic and social development. It planned to pay back the debt through oil sales. But when oil prices dropped in the early 1980s, Mexico found itself $80 billion in debt with not enough money to pay back the loans. It was faced with the worst financial crisis in its history—one from which it is only beginning to recover.

Today, Mexico's economy is a complex mixture of agriculture, industry and international trade. Agriculture is still important, but trade and manufacturing make up the majority of all goods and services produced in a given year.

Most experts agree that while serious problems still exist, current Mexican president Carlos Salinas de Gortari is making great progress toward repairing the severely damaged economy.

Above: **Small cattle ranches are still common in the rural areas of Mexico. Most of these animals will be sold as beef in the markets.**

Opposite: **Mexico's economy is industrializing at a rapid pace because of the availability of skilled and cheap labor.**

Forests cover about one-fifth of Mexico. The valuable wood found in these forests includes ebony, mahogany, rosewood and walnut.

SOURCES OF REVENUE

Mexicans often talk about the extreme generosity God displayed when He created their natural resources: huge amounts of gold, silver and other valuable metals; oil, timber, rivers for irrigation and hydroelectric power; beautiful coastlines to attracts tourists; waters filled with fish and mountains full of game.

MANUFACTURING Mexico's transformation from a primarily agricultural economy to an industrial one is largely due to the relatively new oil industry.

Almost half of Mexico's manufacturing takes place in Mexico City and its suburbs. This area is the country's leading industrial center. Guadalajara and Monterrey are also important industrial cities. The Monterrey Institute of Technology trains some of the country's best engineers.

Mexico's most important products include farming machinery, chemicals, clothing, iron and steel, processed foods, petroleum, beer, rubber, wood pulp and paper. The automobile industry makes cars of good quality for export. The National Railroad Car factory supplies most of the cars and equipment used by Mexico's railway system.

The quick growth of manufacturing in Mexico since the 1940s has affected the entire economy. The production of raw materials for new factories has increased; banking, marketing, and other service industries have expanded.

Heavy government spending on construction has provided additional housing for the growing industrial centers. Power plants have been built to supply the new industries. New highways and railroads were constructed for carrying both raw materials and finished goods.

Inside a steel factory. Mexico's economy today can be described as industrial rather than agricultural.

AGRICULTURE Ever since the early Indians domesticated wild corn, Mexico has been a very agricultural country. Despite the fact that only about one-third of the land can be farmed, many Mexicans must farm to survive and will try to grow crops anywhere they can. It is not unusual, for instance, to see corn growing on a rocky slope.

The kind of crops grown in Mexico varies depending on the altitude, rainfall and temperature of the different regions. However, most of the country is mountainous or receives little rainfall, and is naturally unsuited for growing crops.

The southern part of Mexico's Central Plateau contains the best farmland. The dry northern part of the plateau is used mainly for cattle grazing, although irrigation projects have developed some farmland.

The wet, hot regions of southern and eastern Mexico, and the eastern coastal plains require much work to turn them into productive farmlands. This work includes clearing and draining the land, and controlling floods, insects and plant diseases.

The western coast of Mexico has some areas with fertile soil, but most of it is mountainous and dry.

Mexico is self-sufficient in cotton, which is cultivated mainly in the northwestern part of the country. Sisal fiber, obtained from henequen leaves and used for making rope and rugs, is the major product of the Yucatán area.

Other important agricultural products include corn, oranges, bananas, rice, sugar, potatoes, chilies, coffee, fresh fruit and beans.

Harvesting corn. Corn is grown in many parts of Mexico because it is the staple food of Mexicans.

This was the richest colonial silver mine in Mexico. Today, with the new technology available, it is being reworked again.

MINING Stories of vast amounts gold and silver were what originally attracted Cortés and the Spanish *conquistadors* to Mexico. Today, it still has large amounts of these minerals. The country also has huge deposits of copper, lead, silver, zinc, petroleum, iron ore and sulfur.

The Central Plateau is the country's most heavily mineralized region. Each year, Mexico mines about one-sixth of the world's total production of silver, making it the world's leading producer.

The vast oil reserves in Mexico are the largest in the Western Hemisphere, and are roughly equal to those in Saudi Arabia. As a result, Mexico is also one of the world's leading producers of petroleum, pumping about a billion barrels each year. The petroleum industry is operated by the government.

The Bank of Mexico. One of the biggest problems facing the economy is the repayment of the huge debt it owes to the world's financial institutions.

ELECTRIC POWER Petroleum, natural gas and coal generate about 70% of Mexico's electric power. The other 30% is produced by hydroelectric plants. The government handles almost all of the country's power production and distribution. Chicoasen Dam, Mexico's largest hydroelectric plant and one of the world's highest dams, is located on the Grijalva River in the state of Chiapas.

FOREIGN TRADE Most of Mexico's trade is with the United States, but trade with Western Europe and Japan is increasing. At present, trade with other Latin American countries is relatively insignificant, but the Latin American Integration Association, an economic union of Mexico and 10 other Latin American countries, is working to increase it.

Mexico's major exports reflect the recent changes in the complexity of its economy. Whereas 30 years ago, the leading exports were all food and mineral products: sugar, coffee, tomatoes, lead, copper and zinc, today, exports include processed food, automobiles, chemicals, paper, tires and oil. Petroleum and its industries make up about two-thirds of the exports. The dry rangelands in the northern part of the country are used to raise unfattened cattle, most of which are exported to the United States.

An essential part of the service industry is air transportation.

SERVICE INDUSTRIES As the name suggests, these industries produce services, not products. They play an important part in Mexico's economy, providing about 55% of the total number of jobs.

Some of the larger service industries in Mexico include schools, hospitals, stores, hotels, restaurants, banking, trade and transportation.

TRANSPORTATION

Transportation modes in Mexico range from the modern to the ancient. All major cities and towns are connected by airlines, highways and railroads. But some farmers, especially those in small villages, still carry goods to market on their heads and backs, or by burros or ox-carts, as their forefathers have done for hundreds of years.

Mexico is an important center of international air travel. Guadalajara, Acapulco, Monterrey and Mérida have large international airports. It is also an important seaport. Some of the more important ones are at Coatzacoalcos, Tampico, Veracruz, Guaymas and Salina Cruz.

Mexico's most popular beach resorts include Acapulco, Ensenada, Manzanillo, Mazatlan, Puerto Vallarta, Cancún and Cozumel Island.

TOURISM The tourist trade is extremely vital to Mexico's economy. It is often called "the industry without chimneys." Indeed, the Mexican government promotes tourism as an economic asset.

Four to five million tourists visit Mexico each year. Winter is an especially popular time to visit because of Mexico's warm climate. The most popular destinations are Mexico City, and the ruins of Mayan and Aztec Indian cities.

In the last decade, about 80% of visitors to Mexico were from the United States. In addition, approximately 60 million brief crossings are made each year by Americans for shopping, dining, or auto-repair purposes rather than for actual vacations.

MEXICANS

THE MEXICAN POPULATION is a unique blend of Old and New World peoples. There are some 200 different Indian tribes and ethnic groups, and small groups of pure-blooded Africans and Europeans. The intermingling of races is so varied and the blending so thorough that Mexico maintains no ethnic statistics.

Mexico is an extremely class-conscious society. The Spanish Conquest was followed by centuries of oppression of both the *mestizos* and the Indians. After achieving independence, the new ruling class of Creoles and *mestizos* continued to discriminate against the Indians. Not until after the Revolution of 1910 were efforts made to advance the Indian's position in society, socially and economically. And while the government tries to promote the Indian's accomplishments through books, films and museums, pure-blooded Indians are still treated as social inferiors.

Above: **A regal looking Indian woman. Mexican Indians look distinctively Asian.**

Opposite: **Everywhere in Mexico, friendly faces will greet you.**

Therefore, many Indians have a deep-seated sense of racial inferiority. Although they were the country's earliest settlers, today the Mexican ideal of beauty is the light-skinned, blue-eyed blonde. These feelings could be due to several factors: the poverty and illiteracy among Mexican Indians; their humiliating conquest by the Spanish; and the history of human sacrifices and cannibalism among some of the Indian tribes.

Others think that the inferiority complex stems from their unaggressive personalities. The Indians try to accept life and things the way they find them; the *mestizos* try to dominate and control these. The Indians are community-oriented; the *mestizos* are strongly individualistic. The Indians believe they are controlled by fate and destiny; the *mestizos* respect the qualities of machismo and strong personality.

THE EARLIEST SETTLERS

Archeologists are unable to pinpoint exactly *when* the first Indians arrived in Mesoamerica, but they are able to explain *how* they arrived. It seems the Ice Age created a land bridge from Siberia to Alaska where the Bering Strait is now. Tens of thousands of years ago, bands of nomadic Asians crossed this strip of land in search of food. As the Ice Age ended, the bridge from Siberia melted and was submerged. The migrations stopped. The Asians were in the Americas to stay.

Evidence of Mexico's Asian roots exists even today. Many Mexicans still have Asian features, and in some very fundamental ways Mexico's culture and people are more Oriental than Western.

Olmec head sculptures with African features. Whether people with these features actually lived in Mexico is a mystery. It is believed that the Olmecs had no contact with any foreign civilizations as their languages are unlike those in other parts of the world, and no relics from other civilizations have been found.

THE INDIANS

Mexico still has between 8 to 10 million Indians, divided into 56 recognized ethnic and language groups and speaking over 100 different dialects. Some groups, such as the Nashuas, Mayas, Zapotecs and Mixtecs, number in the hundred thousands and dominate the population of entire regions of the country, though they are often fragmented into small communities. Others, like the Lacandones, Kiliwas, Cucapas and Paispais, have been reduced to a few dozen families. Most have gradually absorbed features of the *mestizo* culture, but some still live in almost total isolation.

Some remote Indian villages are cut off from many modern things such as telephone and electricity. Their lives have remained virtually the same as when Cortés arrived. (For instance, many Indians still sleep on thin straw mats or in hammocks.) These villages form a striking contrast to the sophisticated, cosmopolitan areas of Mexico City and Guadalajara.

In Mexico, Indians and *mestizos* have become very much a part of an integrated society.

Mestizos are people of Spanish and Indian heritage.

MESTIZOS

In contrast to the early colonists of North America, who brought entire families to the New World to start a new life in the hope of escaping religious persecution at home, the Spanish conquerors were adventurers out to claim new lands for themselves and for the Spanish crown.

There was no place for women or children in their often violent and war-like adventures, so they left their families at home. As a result, a great deal of intermarriages between Spanish men and Indian women took place. The children born to these Spanish-Indian couples were the first *mestizos.*

Today, 60% of the Mexican population is *mestizo.* No other former Spanish colony in Latin America is as thoroughly and deeply *mestizo* as Mexico. Large Indian populations still exist in Central and South America, but the ruling classes are usually made up of pure-blooded Europeans.

Although the colonies of other countries in the region were similarly shaped by migrants from Europe and later by slaves from Africa, only in Mexico did complete religious, political and racial mixture take place.

POPULATION PROBLEMS

In 1989, the population of Mexico was estimated to be about 89 million, making it the second most populous country in Latin America and the 11th most populous nation in the world.

Most experts believe that by the year 2000, Mexico's population will be 115 million. Given these numbers, it is not hard to understand why one of the biggest problems facing Mexico's leaders is how to satisfy the basic needs of this enormous population.

Overpopulation leads to unemployment and a drop in housing, health and welfare facilities.

Ironically, much-needed improvements in Mexican health care since 1930 have contributed to the population problem. While infant mortality rates were dropping drastically, the birth rate remained high. The result was a surge in population that made it impossible for the government to keep up with demands for housing, health, education and other social services. However, since birth control was implemented in 1976, the birth rate has dropped dramatically.

COSTUME

In cities and large towns, Mexicans wear clothing similar to that worn in the United States. Those who can afford to will even travel to Paris or New York to buy their clothes. The villagers' clothes, however, are very simple and practical. They are designed to meet the needs of a particular region and climate. Often the designs are hundreds of years old.

In central and southern Mexico, village men usually wear plain cotton shirts and pants, and leather sandals called *huaraches*. Wide-brimmed felt or straw hats called *sombreros* offer them protection from the sun, and *ponchos* protect them from the rain. At night, men wrap themselves in *serapes*, colorful blankets carried over one shoulder during the day.

The village women wear blouses and long, full skirts. They usually go barefoot. They use shawls, which are called *rebozos*, to cover their heads. Mothers also use *rebozos* to wrap their babies to their backs.

Mexican Indians are famous for their beautiful homemade fabrics. Weaving styles are different throughout Mexico, and it is possible to identify an Indian's regional homeland by the colors and designs of his *poncho* or *serape*.

Some Indians have traditional clothing that is usually worn on holidays or for other celebrations. Indians in Oaxaca wear large straw capes. Women on the Isthmus of Tehuantepec wear a wide, lacy white headdress called a *huipil grande* on holidays. Mayan women in the Yucatán wear long, loose white dresses that are embroidered around the neck and bottom hem.

The traditional dress of the people consists of colorfully woven shawls and blankets.

In the villages, it is common to see the men dressed in cotton pants and shirt, *sombrero* and sandals.

Perhaps the best-known of all Indian costumes is the *china poblana*. It is worn by women, most commonly when performing the Mexican hat dance. It consists of a full red and green skirt decorated with beads and other ornaments, a short-sleeved, colorfully-embroidered blouse, and a brightly-colored sash.

LIFESTYLE

BECAUSE THERE IS A VERY BIG difference in Mexico between city life and village life, where a Mexican comes from has a profound effect on the way he or she lives.

Most Mexican cities are cosmopolitan, and the lifestyles reflect those in many American and European cities. Values are generally more liberal than they are in the villages. Women have far more opportunities, jobs are easier to find, and education and health care are more accessible.

In contrast, life on the farms and in the villages has changed very little over the last 100 years. Many farmers live in small villages located near their fields. Some Indians resent the imposition of the *mestizo* culture. They still follow their ancient customs and live as their ancestors did before the Spanish arrived.

A large number of Mexican cities and towns began as Indian communities. After the Spaniards arrived, they rebuilt the communities and made them more like Spanish towns. The central church and main public and government buildings were built around a public square called a plaza. The plazas were meant to serve as the center of city life.

In addition to a plaza, almost every village, city and town in Mexico has a marketplace. Going to market is an important activity for the people in farm areas. Men, women and children take whatever they wish to sell or trade, and either rent stalls in which to display their goods, or spread their merchandise on the ground. Then they spend the day at the market visiting with friends or selling their wares.

Above: **In the rural areas of Mexico, the lifestyle has not changed much since the beginning of this century.**

Opposite: **The Independence Statue in Mexico City. By the year 2000, it is estimated that Mexico City will have a population of 25 million people.**

53

The average Mexican family consists of about five or six persons, the father being the bread-winner and, often, the head of the family.

FAMILY: THE CORE OF SOCIETY

Mexican families form the very core of the country's society. Indeed, the strength of the family forms the foundation of Mexico's continued political stability.

In Mexico, the word *family* means not just immediate family, but also includes the extended family—aunts, uncles and cousins. The family is extremely self-sufficient and very much closed to outsiders, except for very close friends who are considered part of the family. The extended

54

family provides a crucial support structure, both emotionally and economically, to each of its members. Family-run farms, stores, shops, restaurants and other small businesses employ millions of people. Even the poorest families offer their members more economic security in times of hardship than the government.

Family members' social lives revolve around being with relatives. Children have so many brothers, sisters and cousins that they have virtually no need for any other friends!

The Mexican family structure has survived a great deal of upheaval in the last 50 years. The population explosion forced sons and daughters of rural families to leave home in search of work. Children of middle-class and wealthy families began to travel much more than

Older sisters are often required to help the mother in looking after her younger siblings.

their parents did, learning foreign languages and adopting foreign fashions. Industrialization and urbanization drastically restructured provincial lifestyles. And the Catholic Church lost much of its influence as people became less religious. But through it all the family survived. Today, over 90% of Mexicans still live with their families.

The average Mexican household consists of five or six people. Often, several generations of the same family live together. The head of the family is the grandfather or great-grandfather. The father is the unquestioned figure of authority. Unfortunately, sometimes his job or his machismo leads him to neglect his wife and family as he feels that the task of keeping the home is solely a woman's duty. A mother is usually adored by her children as she is the one who showers all the care and attention on them.

RITES OF PASSAGE

CHILDHOOD AND ADOLESCENCE Mexican girls do not have nearly as much freedom as American girls. Peasant girls are assigned household chores from the time they are very young, and by the time they are seven or eight, most are helping to care for their younger brothers and sisters. It is not unusual in Mexican villages to see little girls with babies strapped to their backs.

Rural peasants view cities as centers of sin, and consequently are extremely reluctant to allow their daughters to go there. The only possible exception might be if the girl has a cousin or aunt already established in the city who lets the young girl live with her. Mexican boys are usually doted upon by their mothers. They are allowed more independence and time as they are free from household chores. In the villages, though, sons normally help in the fields.

Social and economic pressures require most young men and women to live at home until they are married. Many daughters of wealthy families may live and study abroad. Yet upon their return, they go back to their parents' home.

MARRIAGE Marriage in the Indian villages is still very old-fashioned and traditional. Village girls usually marry between the ages of 14 and 16, and village boys in their late teens. Marriages are still arranged in some Indian communities, and the bride's family is expected to provide a dowry.

In the rural southeast, custom requires that the male members of a family object to a woman's leaving home. Thus, she is often taken by force by her boyfriend, with peace eventually restored between the families only after their first child is born.

Huichol girls marry when they are as young as 13. Men commonly have more than one wife and adultery is tolerated.

Poor Mexicans usually cannot afford the fee for a marriage license, but they still live together as husband and wife. These marriages are considered valid in the eyes of their peers. Some Indians wear feathers of small birds in their hair to indicate their married status.

PREGNANCY AND CHILDBIRTH Mexicans believe that viewing birth as a beginning and death as an end leaves one with no sense of a living past. Therefore, neither birth nor death is seen to interrupt the continuity of life, and neither is considered very important.

Most women become pregnant shortly after getting married. If an unmarried village girl becomes pregnant, the father of her child will usually marry her. This is not the case, however, in the cities. Consequently, the number of unwed mothers is much higher in urban areas.

A funeral in procession. The people believe that the spirit or soul of a person never dies.

DEATH AND FUNERALS Mexicans celebrate the Day of the Dead every November by having picnics at cemeteries and eating on the graves of their ancestors as they believe the departed souls return on that day. The belief in the ability to communicate with the dead is also widespread. It is an outgrowth of the view that the past is never dead. Death to the Mexican is not the end, but only one phase in an infinite cycle.

Mexican feelings about death go back to the religion of the Aztecs, and were reinforced by Catholicism. The Aztecs believed that the death of the sacrificial victim had great significance. The Catholics believed the same thing about the individual, although they also believed that what happened to the individual after he dies is determined largely by the way he lived. Catholics shifted the emphasis in attitudes toward death, but did not significantly alter them.

MACHISMO

Machismo is basically a strong sense of masculine pride among many Mexican men. They are constantly trying to prove their manhood. Typical things these men do include having mistresses in addition to their wives, being domineering and overly protective of the women around them,

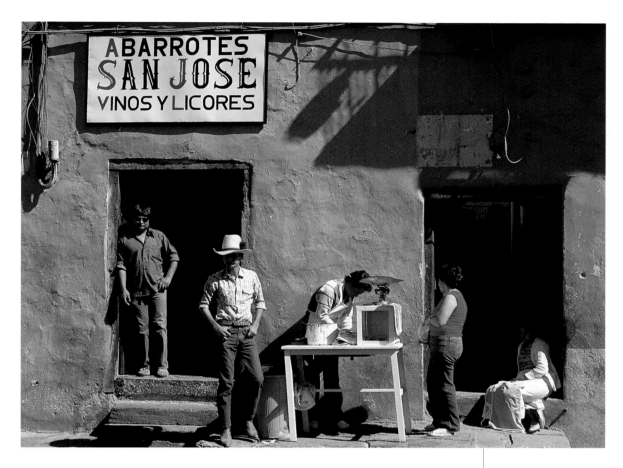

picking up the checks in restaurants even when they cannot afford it, and producing lots of children. They must be aggressive and project an image of strength. Most agree that machismo is a front behind which these men hide their insecurities and fears. They try to cover up with pride and gutsiness.

Perhaps the most damaging effect of machismo is in the men's treatment of women and in their adulterous ways. Machismo has ruined countless marriages. Another damaging effect is the resulting pregnancies, which partly explains why Mexico has the highest birth rate in the world.

Ironically, together with this attitude is a non-macho characteristic. These same men can be extremely tender with children and affectionate toward friends. Even the most macho of men may cry in public.

Machismo requires a man to be aggressive and project an image of strength.

It is common for young
girls to help the family
out, especially in the
home or even the family
business.

WOMEN

Although women in Mexico are generally treated as second-class citizens, their role in society is crucial. Despite all the bravado of the Mexican machismo, Mexican women are the pillars of the family. They are the ones who pass on to their children religious beliefs, legends and customs that are so important to family and community life.

Mexico is less liberal in its attitudes toward women than, for example, the United States. In Mexico, a woman's principal attributes are thought to be her beauty, compassion and tenderness. She is supposed to give her husband obedience, pleasure, assistance and counsel, and is expected to always treat him with the respect due to somebody who supports and defends her.

As is the case in most Latin American countries, peasant women in Mexico do very little outside the home besides go to market. At home, they prepare the food, wash the clothes and raise the children. They usually have many children, not only because birth control is almost

non-existent, but because they need the extra hands to help with the work, and the security of having many providers for them when they grow old. Their traditional husbands may also believe it is important to produce a lot of children to show their manliness.

Peasant women rarely talk to strangers, and would never join their husbands at the table with a visitor. The only exception might be grandmothers, especially those whose husbands have died. They are revered and are allowed to do "unladylike" things in public such as drinking and smoking.

In urban areas, middle and upper-class women have much more freedom than those from poorer families. Economic conditions have made it necessary for more women to go to work. Having jobs gives them the freedom to leave unhappy marriages that they might otherwise have been forced to maintain. There has also been a steady increase in the number of women attending universities, which has enabled them to get higher-income jobs in the public and private sectors.

CUSTOMS

GREETINGS AND FAREWELLS In Mexico, greetings and goodbyes are quite warm and affectionate, and always involve a handshake. Women kiss each other on the cheek when introduced and whenever they meet. These formalities are very important, and it is considered rude not to do them. The main form of greeting, especially between men, is the *abrazo*, or embrace. It follows a strict pattern. First comes the handshake, followed by the embrace and two strong coordinated pats on the back, and finally, a second handshake and a pat on the shoulder.

COMPADRES AND COMADRES Literally translated, they mean co-mother and co-father. These people are comparable to the godmother and godfather in the United States. *Compadres* and *comadres* often support each other in times of need, broadening the family network and tightening the social structure, especially in poorer communities. Younger people are more casual about whom they call *compadre*, and sometimes give the name to their close friends.

THE *MANANA* SYNDROME Mexicans have their own unique sense of time. It can be very frustrating to people who are unfamiliar with it. Usually, they are either hours late for appointments, or they never show up at all. They believe anything enjoyable at the moment is not worth ending for the sake of a future appointment.

It is also almost impossible for Mexicans to say "no." They accept invitations and make appointments that they have no intention of keeping, because they believe it is ruder to refuse an invitation than to not show up. This attitude is referred to as the *mañana* syndrome.

Mexicans are a very warm, polite and helpful people.

POLITENESS Mexicans are a very polite people. When answering the question, "Where are you from," they will often say *"donde tiene su casa"* or "where your home is," implying that "my home is your home." One must be careful when admiring another's possessions. The owner of the item often will offer it to the admirer as a gift and envy is a discouraged emotion among Mexicans.

SIESTAS Most Mexicans living in villages and rural areas eat a big meal, called a *comida,* in the afternoon, and take a nap, or *siesta,* until about 4 p.m. During this time, shops close and things become very quiet. Schoolchildren also go home for a *siesta*, and return in the afternoon. The hectic schedules of people in the city are steadily eliminating this custom.

SOCIAL CONDITIONS

Mexico has an elite class of wealthy citizens who have lifestyles comparable to the elite of any country. It also has a fairly large middle class. But the majority of the population live in degrees of poverty that range from just making do to starvation. While Mexico is more formally committed to improving its social conditions—its government spends billions of dollars annually on social welfare programs—real progress has yet to be felt.

HEALTH Although social assistance and health services have greatly reduced the death rate over the last 60 years, the health of the rural and urban poor is still far below the government's minimum standards. Malnutrition is extremely common and has caused a high number of diseases such as rickets, vitamin deficiency and anemia. There are also many cases of tonsilitis, influenza and respiratory diseases, all of which are hard to control. The Mexican's average life span is about five years less than that of the American.

Spanish is the language of instruction in schools.

HOUSING The housing crisis, particularly in the cities, is one of the most serious of Mexico's social problems. In addition to a serious housing shortage, housing conditions for two-thirds of the population are poor; they have insufficient water supply, poor drainage, or other defects.

WELFARE SERVICES Mexico has no unemployment or welfare benefits. If people don't have jobs, they must improvise or rely on their families to get them through.

EDUCATION Since the Revolution, Mexico has invested large amounts of money in its education system, successfully helping many Mexicans improve their lives. But the growing population is leaving the educational system with many problems. Sadly, the average Mexican attends school for only five years, and 15% of adults are illiterate.

WAGES AND COST OF LIVING Mexicans are some of the hardest and most tireless workers in the world. The average Mexican man must work from dawn to dusk just to survive, and even then, his wages are barely enough to support his family. Luxuries often require that women and children work as well.

A 1934 law requiring employers to pay a minimum wage is rarely observed. Even workers fortunate enough to earn the minimum wage are unable to feed or house their families decently. Workers are entitled to ask for a raise twice a year, but the typical increase in wages rarely covers the increase in cost of living.

In the villages, there are no asphalt roads, proper drains or running water.

A new middle-class housing complex with all the facilities of a modern home.

CASA MEXICANA

Mexican suburbs are full of modern houses and apartment buildings. The older parts of the cities have rows of Spanish colonial-style homes. Most of these houses are made of stone or adobe brick. Spanish-style homes have patios, which are located at the center of the building and serve as the center of family life.

The poorest Mexicans live in slum shacks or rooms with almost no furniture. *Petates* (straw mats) serve as beds, and clay bowls as dishes. Entire families might live in a one-room house. The shapes, styles and building materials of these homes vary according to the requirements of the climate. Those on the dry Central Plateau are made of adobe, cement blocks or stones, with flat roofs of red tiles, sheet metal or straw. Some have hard-packed dirt floors, one door, and few or no windows. Cooking is done in a kitchen against an outside wall or over a fire on the floor.

In areas with a lot of rain, most houses have walls of poles covered with a mixture of lime and clay. This mixture lasts longer in the rain than adobe does. The houses have sloping roofs to allow the water to run off easily. In Yucatán, most Indian houses are rectangular with rounded ends, and roofs are made of neatly trimmed palm leaves.

MEXICO CITY

Mexico City is the capital of the nation and is one of the largest cities in the world. It was founded soon after the conquest of Mexico at the site of Tenochtitlán, the Aztec capital. Before Mexico's independence, it served as the capital of New Spain, was captured by American troops during the Mexican War, conquered by the French army, and captured by rebel forces during the Mexican Revolution.

Mexico City always surprises visitors with its sophistication and European air. It is a culturally rich, dynamic city full of Aztec ruins, colonial buildings, beautiful parks, superb shopping malls and excellent museums. But co-existing with all this is some of the worst poverty in all of Mexico.

In recent years, the city has developed a terrible pollution problem. The millions of cars, trucks and buses that swarm the city, and the excessive exhaust and pollutants they produce are trapped in the bowl-shaped valley that holds Mexico City.

RELIGION

THE FIRST INDIANS in Mexico were hunter-gatherers from Asia who crossed the Bering Strait tens of thousands of years ago. When climate changes killed off their existing food source, they were forced to cultivate the land. This was so important to them that they began worshiping gods whom they believed would provide rain and protect their harvests.

From then on, the Indians were dominated by religion. At times, their gods numbered in the hundreds. Indian religion was full of superstitions. Their gods could be good, or they could be cruel. Some believed in the ritualistic killing of human beings to satisfy these gods, and they built huge temples and pyramids to honor them.

Above: **Pictures of Catholic saints. Religious pictures, statues and rituals reflect upon the strong faith of the people.**

Opposite: **The grand and imposing churches built in the 18th and 19th centuries remind us of the past power and wealth of the clergy.**

After the Spanish Conquest, missionaries came from Spain to convert the natives to Catholicism. These men often traveled over harsh terrain to the remotest villages as part of their mission. Converting the Indians was fairly easy, in part because of certain similarities between the two religions, and in part because of the intelligence of the missionaries.

Realizing they had a better chance of success if they compromised, the missionaries allowed the Indians to keep some of their own religious traditions. They also built churches on or near the sites of the temples, enabling the Indians to continue their traditional pilgrimages. The Indians' belief in many gods made it easy for them to accept the Catholic tradition of many saints. Gradually, the Indians in the more populated areas, believing that their gods had also been defeated by the Spaniards, began to accept the Spaniards' god.

The early missionaries were so successful in converting the people that beautiful churches or quaint little chapels can be found in almost every village in Mexico.

ANTI-CHURCH REFORMS

The Catholic Church since the Mexican Revolution has held a very uncertain position in Mexican society. From the time it arrived in Mexico, the Church exploited and oppressed the natives. During the War of Independence, the Catholic Church, afraid of losing its status or power, backed the conservatives. When independence from Spain was finally achieved, the new government began enacting anti-Catholic legislation, a practice which hit its peak during the presidency of Benito Juárez.

The constitution of 1917 contains an enormous number of anti-Church provisions. No religion has any legal status. Men and women must be married in a civil service before they can have a religious ceremony. Land and buildings that once belonged to the Catholic Church are now state property, and government approval is needed before they can be altered or added to. No church leader is allowed to make a political statement in public. Priests must be native-born Mexicans, but they are not allowed to vote, nor are they allowed to wear their clerical robes in public. The number of men who can become priests is limited by the government.

THE VIRGIN OF GUADALUPE

Although there is no proof or documentation, the miracle of the Virgin of Guadalupe is widely believed by the faithful in Mexico.

According to legend, a poor Indian named Juan Diego saw the Virgin of Guadalupe on his way to church one day shortly after he had converted to Catholicism. She appeared as an Indian maiden on Tepeyac Hill at La Villa, just outside Mexico City. She asked Diego to tell the local bishop to build a shrine in her honor on the hill, so that she could protect the Indians with her love. The bishop, however, was skeptical of Diego's story.

The next day, the Virgin appeared again. When Diego told the bishop about this, he demanded proof. When the Virgin appeared for a third time, Diego told her about the bishop's request for proof. She told him to collect roses from a spot on the hill where roses had never grown before. Diego wrapped the roses in a blanket and brought them to the bishop. When he unwrapped the parcel, they both saw the image of the Virgin imprinted on the inside of the cloth. The bishop then built the shrine and placed the cloth in it.

The Basilica of the Virgin of Guadalupe was rebuilt in 1976. The construction was financed by the government, a remarkable gesture considering its official anti-Church stance. The government's involvement is further proof of the importance of the Virgin to Mexican lives. In 1990, Juan Diego was made holy by Pope John Paul II during his visit to Mexico.

Re-enacting the crucifixion of Jesus Christ. Many people make sacrifices before the celebration of Easter to atone for their sins.

THE CHURCH TODAY

Despite their best efforts, the Spanish missionaries were not able to completely rid the Indians of all their beliefs. Superstitions, nature, magic and mystery remained an important part of their religion. Even today, some Indians living in remote villages still worship their ancient ancestral gods. Most Mexicans, however, practice folk Catholicism that combines elements of both religions.

Though the Church as an institution has weakened, religious beliefs are still an integral part of Mexican lives; village priests are often powerful community leaders; and husband-wife relationships are still based on the teachings of the Bible and the Church.

Although 90% of Mexico is Catholic, it is rapidly losing ground to evangelical groups. Between 1950 and 1980, the number of Protestants jumped by more than 500%. Church attendance, especially in urban areas, is dropping, as is the ratio of priests to population. Divorce is becoming more accepted and many people use birth control: both actions are violations of Catholic laws. Abortion is fairly common, although the Church has successfully blocked efforts to legalize it.

In 1990, Pope John Paul II visited Mexico to try to strengthen relations

between the government and the Catholic Church. Although hundreds of thousands of people came to see him, the crowds were much smaller than predicted.

While the laws enacted after the Mexican Revolution used to be strictly enforced, things are much more relaxed today. The overwhelming Catholic nature of the voting population makes current political leaders unwilling to strongly enforce the rules. Many of these leaders are devout Catholics themselves; some have even sent their children to mission schools.

During Pope John Paul II's 1990 visit, he was met at the airport by President Salinas and allowed to wear his clerical robes and say Mass in public. There are many foreign priests in Mexico, despite laws against this, because of the shortage of native-born priests. And Church leaders do at times publicly speak out against the government, even in the press. In general, though, most priests keep a low profile.

LANGUAGE

MOST MEXICANS SPEAK SPANISH, the official language of almost every Latin American country. In fact, Mexico has the largest Spanish-speaking population in the world.

However, the Spanish spoken in Mexico is different from that in Spain, much the way the English spoken in the United States is different from the English spoken in England. Mexican Spanish is a hybrid of Spanish, Indian and some English.

The vocabulary, usage and pronunciation can all be different. Mexican Spanish is a very expressive language. Perhaps nowhere in Latin America is the use of Spanish so deep in meaning.

Speaking indirectly to avoid trouble or commitments has led to a remarkable creativity by Mexicans in the use of their language. Many words have double meanings that would not be known to someone unfamiliar with the language. Excessive frankness or directness is considered rude, and even serious discussions must be preceded by small talk about family or political gossip.

Another curious trait of the Mexicans is the way they use their language to protect themselves. They will make up answers to questions, give themselves titles they don't really have, or simply deny responsibility for their mistakes.

Many words used in the United States come from Spanish. Among them are canyon, corral, desperado, lariat, lasso, patio, rodeo and stampede.

Above: **Mexicans read and write in Spanish.**

Opposite: **Magazines and newspapers in Spanish and English are sold by the streets of the bigger cities in Mexico.**

INDIAN LANGUAGES

The most commonly spoken Indian language is Nahuatl, the language of the Aztecs. The next most common are the Mixtec, Mayan, Zapotec and Otomi languages. These languages can be very different from each other, with many words bearing no similarities at all.

While millions of Mexican Indians primarily use their language in daily life, most also speak Spanish. Today, there are almost 100 active Indian dialects in Mexico. Some dialects, though, are spoken by only a few individuals.

The Spanish thought they could accelerate the natives' integration into Mexican society by eliminating the Indian languages. Their effort basically failed, although it is estimated that as many as 93 Indian languages have disappeared since the Spanish Conquest.

Government policy today no longer forces the Spanish language on the Indians. For instance, when the government began a war against illiteracy in 1944, it provided Indians with important information written in their own languages. This tactic was very successful.

But once the Indians realized how much they could help themselves with Spanish, many learned Spanish. Television and radio have added to the Indians' incentive to learn Spanish. Even the most remote villages have access to this media. So most Indians have become part of the Spanish-speaking community without giving up their own unique talents and skills.

COMMISSION FOR THE DEFENSE OF SPANISH

The government of Mexico tries very hard to maintain its cultural independence from the United States. In the early 1980s, it noticed that more and more English words were creeping into the Spanish language. People were calling themselves Charlie instead of Carlos, or Paul instead of Paco. Owners of restaurants and shops, thinking foreign words were good for business, began naming their establishments Shirley's and Arthur's. It upset some politicians that more and more of these things were creeping into the Spanish language.

In 1982, the government created the Commission for the Defense of the Spanish Language. The commission's purpose was to prevent English from being mixed with the Spanish language. It declared war on the apostrophe—which does not exist in Spanish—as the principal symbol of cultural mixture. It also made radio and television commercials which mocked those who used English phrases. However, the commission's impact has been slight.

HEY AMIGO!

FORMALITIES AND TITLES Mexicans have two ways of saying "you." *Tu* is the familiar form used when greeting friends. *Usted* is the formal version. Mexicans are very strict about when which form is used. It is considered impolite and even rude to use *tu* when greeting a stranger, an elder, or someone who has more authority or is in a higher position.

NICKNAMES These are very common. Most are simply versions of proper names, as in Tonio from Antonio. Many are derived from people's physical characteristics, personalities or jobs. Someone who is overweight could be called *Gordo*, or fatty, and someone with a big nose might be nicknamed *Chato*, or nose. "Junior" is an insulting nickname for those whose status comes from the power or money their parents have. Current president Carlos Salinas de Gortari is a "political junior" because his father, a powerful government official, gave him his start in politics.

These typists in Mexico City provide a service to people who are unable to write or type.

CLASS EUPHEMISMS Although they deny the existence of racial discrimination, many upper-class Mexicans have developed a vocabulary as a subtle way of indicating one's position in society.

Wealthy Mexicans are *gente de razon*, or people of reason. The opposite of the *gente de razon* are the *gente indigena*, or the Indians. Some *mestizos* call themselves *cristianosas* to indicate that they are not Indians. The poor, even if they are *mestizo*, are referred to as *indios* or *inditos*, which literally means Indian, but is actually an insulting term.

SLANG This is an important method of communication in Mexico, and for those unfamiliar with it, it can be difficult to understand. For example, people refer to "the other side" for the United States, "ships" for cars and "wool" for money. Other words may be quite ordinary in other Spanish-speaking countries, but are considered swear words in Mexico.

MALINCHISMO This is the Mexican word for traitor, or for one who rejects his own cultural heritage for foreign things. It comes from the name of an Indian maiden, Malinche, who served as one of Hernán Cortés's translators. Through Malinche and another translator who was Spanish, Cortés was able to form alliances with Indians that were critical to the success of the Spanish Conquest. To this day, Malinche holds a place in Mexican history equivalent to the place Benedict Arnold holds in American history.

The use of informal language or slang is common among friends.

NON-VERBAL LANGUAGE

1. *Ojo* (Eye). A way of warning someone to "be careful" or of indicating "he's shrewd."
2. *Quien Sabe?* (Who knows?) This gesture is usually accompanied by raised eyebrows, facial contortions and groans. It means "I take no responsibility."
3. *Las uñas* (fingernails). Can refer either to a thief or to a theft. Often used as a warning that a known thief is near by, or as a way of explaining that something was stolen.
4. Used to indicate the height of inanimate objects.
5. Used to indicate the height of animals.
6. Used to indicate the height of people (it can be insulting to use either 4 or 5 when referring to the height of people).
7. *Lana* (money). A way of saying something is expensive.
8. *Ijole!* (Wow!) The fingers should make a noticeable pop.
9. *No, Ni modos* (No, no way).
10. *Adelante* (ahead). This is a very common gesture, and to those unfamiliar with it, it can be very confusing. It means "come here" or "move forward," but looks like "go away."
11. *Momentito, aboritita* (a moment). A signal that means not much, a little bit or even "I'll be right back." It is often used in place of a verbal promise that one knows cannot be fulfilled.
12. *No, gracias* (No, thank you). Used much the way it is used in the United States as a sign of appreciation when turning something down.

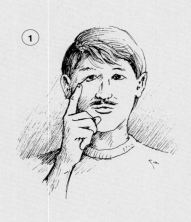

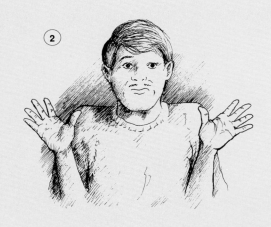

THE ARTS

MEXICO HAS ONE OF THE MOST ancient, continuous and important artistic heritages of any region in the Americas.

Mexican art is a combination of forms from ancient Indian civilizations, Spanish colonialism, Catholicism, and the revolutionary political ideas of the last hundred years.

Mexican Indian art before the age of Columbus (known as pre-Columbian art) is as interesting to historians and archeologists as it is to art lovers. Created by the Indians in isolation with virtually no outside influence, it achieved a remarkable level of development and sophistication.

When the Spaniards arrived, Indian culture still survived, but Mexican forms of writing, painting, music and architecture began to be influenced and dominated by European styles. After the Mexican Revolution, the country began to use its culture to promote a sense of national identity. Art became a powerful medium for patriotism.

Today, the artistic expression of the country remains uniquely Mexican, but is freer than in the past. Artists are able to develop new techniques that are drawn from the artistic traditions of other countries and to address themes by using Mexico and its culture as a form of inspiration.

Above: **The blend of Spanish and Indian architectural styles can be seen in the façades of the many old colonial churches.**

Opposite: **The great city of Tenochtitlán. This mural by Diego Rivera reflects the rediscovery of and the renewed pride over Mexico's ancient heritage.**

83

PRE-COLUMBIAN ART AND ARCHITECTURE

Not surprisingly, most pre-Columbian art is religious. The ancient Indians' lives were dominated by their gods, and much of their art was created to please them or simply used as peace offerings.

The Olmec Indians, who developed the first civilized culture in Mexico, were also the country's first real artists. They are best known for their beautiful, intricate stone carvings. The huge carvings of heads are the earliest portraits of these ancient people. The Olmecs were also the first people to make jewelry and ceramics.

The Olmecs were the inventors of the pyramid, which would become so important in every culture that followed. What started out as mounds of earth covered with rough stones developed into some of the most beautiful structures of all time. These pyramids served several functions: they were temples where priests could pray and perform rituals, and they were symbolic mountains meant to bring the Indians closer to heaven. The Pyramid of the Niches in Tajín is one of the most magnificent in all of Mexico.

The Mayans excelled in all artistic areas but are especially known for the beauty of their ceramics. The Mayan cities of Palenque, Chichén Itza and Uxmal are rich with Mayan art. Teotihuacán contained extraordinary pyramids, temples and roads made for kings.

The last native empire, the Aztec, founded a magnificent capital, Tenochtitlán, on the site of present-day Mexico City. Tenochtitlán's architecture and art reflect its inhabitants' harsh religion through carved depictions of human sacrifices.

The Indians considered skill in art a moral virtue,

The Aztec Sunstone is a remarkable work of art and science. The Sunstone is actually used as a calendar to calculate the number of days in a year.

and one of the ways of being religious. Their accomplishments are even more remarkable considering that they did not have any iron tools with which to carve their sculptures or erect their pyramids.

When the Spaniards arrived, they were stunned by the highly-developed nature of the natives' art and architecture. They also believed much of this art was the work of the devil, and did everything they could to destroy it. They melted down gold objects, shattered sacred sculptures, and burned many things. Some of it survived, but one can only imagine the magnificent things that were destroyed.

The Pyramid of the Magician in Uxmal was built by the Mayans without any iron tools to carve or erect the stones.

POST-REVOLUTIONARY ART AND THE MURALISTS

The 1910 Revolution had a dramatic effect on Mexican art. Artists became patriotic and their works had a strong political tone. They used realistic techniques to depict contemporary political conflicts. The Revolution also inspired a group of young painters to search for a style to incorporate the great pre-Columbian native art. They felt that their art must be "of the people." They decided the best way to do both was by painting vast murals in public buildings. Three Mexicans are considered the giants of the muralist movement: Diego Rivera, David Siqueiros and José Orozco. Together, they transformed the Mexican art world.

Rivera was the founder. Inspired by native art and his experiences in Europe, he painted large murals dealing with Mexican life, history and social problems. Siqueiros was a political activist. He fought in the Revolution, volunteered to fight in the Spanish Civil War, took part in labor struggles and was imprisoned several times. His murals focused on social protests.

Orozco is considered the best Mexican muralist of all time. While Rivera and Siqueiros were noted for their artistic works in other forms like easel painting and sculpture, Orozco was at his best with murals. His work, which has been called the least Mexican of the three, reflects his deep political feelings and a search for deep and universal symbols.

THE ART SCENE TODAY

For the most part, the art world has not given Mexican artists the attention they deserve. Although there is some recognition for Mexican muralists like Diego Rivera, contemporary Mexican artists such as José Fors, Manuel Gonzalez Serrano, Alicia Rahon, Ricardo Martinez and José Orozco are largely unknown outside their country.

Indian artistic influences can be found today almost everywhere in Mexico—in interior decoration, architecture, jewelry, coins, clothing design and advertising. Mexicans seem to be rediscovering the beauty of their native Indian art, or at least developing a respect for it.

Budding artists at work. People all over the world are slowly rediscovering the unique beauty of Mexican art.

CRAFTS AND FOLK ARTS

Crafts and folk arts have flourished throughout Mexican history, and despite increased modernization of Mexican society, they still make up a vital part of the nation's life and economy. When Mexicans eat, dress, play, or pray, they are using crafts with long histories and strong traditions.

Many contemporary crafts continue ancient Indian traditions. As in pre-Spanish Mexico, pottery is a major activity, and much of it is still made by hand without the use of a wheel. Weaving is still frequently done on a backstrap loom. *Huipils* (pronounced "wee-peels"), long

Local pottery on sale. In some places the art of pottery has not changed since the pre-Spanish days.

blouses, *quexquemetls* (pronounced "kesh-kay-meh-tahls") and capes, worn in the past by Indian women, are still woven today, and worn on occasions like weddings or fiestas.

The Spanish influence on Mexican crafts has been significant. Wool was unknown in ancient Mexico until the introduction of sheep into the Americas. *Serapes* (blankets), *rebozos* (shawls) and techniques such as glazing resulted from Spanish influence.

MUSIC

Music was everywhere in the culture of Mexico's early Indians. They believed that it kept the world in motion and nature on their side. All Indian ceremonies involved music. Music was also educational, and the Indians used it to pass their history from generation to generation.

The instruments the Indians used were whistles, flutes, percussion instruments, drums, giant conch shells, rattles, trumpets, and notched deer bones. The earliest instruments date from about 1500 B.C. and were made of bone, wood, animal hide or baked clay.

The Spanish *conquistadors* vigilantly pursued the destruction of Indian music, which they thought was inspired by the devil. Their efforts failed, in part because Spanish priests found it easier to convert the Indians if they were allowed to transfer their ceremonial use of music from Indian deities to Catholic ones. Today, Indians in some parts of Mexico still play their ancestors' music.

A popular style of Mexican music is *nortena*, which combines elements of *corridos*—or ballads—with waltzes and polkas. It was brought over by the thousands of Eastern Europeans and Germans who immigrated in the mid-19th century. But the musicians perhaps most associated with Mexico today are the *mariachis*. *Mariachi* groups can have anywhere from three to over a dozen musicians. They wear big *sombreros*, tight dark suits covered with silver, frilly shirts and cowboy boots. Their music is dominated by guitars and violins, and they play mostly romantic, sentimental songs.

In Mexico City, *mariachi* groups gather and play to each other at Garibaldi Square, hoping to be hired by passers-by. It is a Mexican tradition for suitors to hire *mariachis* to serenade their lovers, or for husbands to hire them to serenade their wives. The most popular serenading hours are between 2 and 4 in the morning. These musicians play at virtually all Mexican parties, weddings and public fiestas.

Strolling *mariachi* groups stop under windows of apartment buildings, while organ-grinders and guitarists walk into restaurants and buses to serenade prospective clients who may wish to hire them.

The Feast of the Virgin of Guadalupe. Most of Mexico's dances were religious in origin and purpose; now, however, almost all are secular and performed at fiestas or for the sheer delight of dancing.

DANCE

Dance was as important to the ancient Indians as music. Like music, it was highly religious; the Aztecs and Mayans never danced for any reason other than to communicate with their gods. They had dances to bring them luck in almost everything they did, including hunting, marriage, war and harvest. The participants in the dance would wear special dresses. In their never-ending quest to destroy the Indian culture, the Spanish conquerors forbade community dancing, but this also failed.

THE *VOLODORES*

Probably the most spectacular of all early dances is the *volodores*, or flying pole dance. It is an ancient rain dance.

Four men wearing feathered costumes are tightly secured by ropes to a 100-foot pole. They represent the four seasons. Another man is seated on a small platform on top of the pole, playing an instrument. The four men with ropes drop off the pole and swing around 13 times before they reach the ground. The total number of rotations, which is 52, represents the number of weeks in a year. The *volodores* is still re-enacted in various villages.

The most beautiful and powerful dances today are pre-Spanish Conquest in origin. The deer dance of the Yaqui Indians is popular all over Mexico. Originally performed to court luck in hunting, it is now featured at many religious fiestas and ceremonies. This exciting dance depicts the chase and killing of a deer, with all the dancers portraying animals with amazing realism. Another favorite is the Sandunga dance from Tehuantepec, which is known for its beautiful music.

One of the few colorful dances introduced after the Spanish Conquest is the *los moros*, about the war between Moors and Christians. It is performed at bullfights and other celebrations. Half the dancers dress as Moors, and the other half as Christians. *Los moros*, which can be performed with a thousand men, usually involves about a dozen. It remains one of the most popular ritual dances today, especially around the Federal District and central states.

The Mexican hat dance is a popular national folk dance recognized by people around the world.

MODERN ARCHITECTURE

After wiping out as much as they could of the pre-Columbian art forms, the Spanish taught the Indians to use European art and building techniques. The result was a new style that combined European and indigenous Indian styles.

The development of modern architecture in Mexico in many ways paralleled that of Mexican painting. The tradition of grand art that stretched back to pre-Spanish times culminated with the dictator Porfirio Díaz. Díaz was responsible for building the Palace of Fine Arts and the Congress building. After the 1920s, architecture adjusted to the political mood of nationalism. The state constructed large buildings decorated with murals and sculptures. As with painting, Mexican architecture then entered a great period in the 1950s, achieving dramatic and exciting results by blending many of the colors and shapes of traditional Mexico with modern styles and techniques imported from abroad.

LITERATURE

Carlos Fuentes is the best known of Mexico's contemporary writers. Two of his major novels, *The Death of Artemio Cruz* and *Where the Air is Clear*, have been widely translated. They portray the upper—and often seamier—side of Mexican society and politics.

Octavio Paz is a poet noted for his insight, elegance and knowledge. One of his most famous works is *The Labyrinth of Solitude: Life and Thought in Mexico*. In it, he does much to clarify the Mexican character. In 1990, Paz became the first native-born Mexican to receive the Nobel Prize for literature.

A surprising number of well-known British and American authors have written about or set the plots of some of their best novels in Mexico. They include Saul Bellow, Ray Bradbury, Graham Greene, Jack Kerouac, D.H. Lawrence, Jack London, Katherine Porter, Oscar Lewis and John Steinbeck.

The National Library in Mexico City.

LEISURE

LIKE ALMOST EVERYTHING ELSE in Mexico, leisure time is determined by one's status in society. Mexico's wealthy spend it the same way the rich in the United States do: dining out, traveling, and playing "country club sports." Those who can afford it think nothing of flying off to Houston, Los Angeles, or New York when they feel like it. The poor, on the other hand, must work from dawn to dark just to make a living. For them, fiestas are their only luxury.

Sunday is the most leisurely day of the week in Mexico. It is an important family day. Favorite activities include picnics, family get-togethers, attending bullfights and, in smaller towns, courtship around the town square.

Opposite: **Diving off the cliffs at Acapulco.**

Left: **Many young people and families enjoy going to amusement parks.**

The grand Plaza de Tores in Mexico City is the largest bullfighting stadium in the world.

THE BULLFIGHT

Bullfighting was brought to Mexico by the Spaniards shortly after the Conquest. For the next 300 years that Mexico was a colony, bullfights were held regularly to commemorate religious and civic celebrations. Today, bullfighting is one of Mexico's most popular spectator activities. Mexico City's bullfighting ring, the Plaza de Tores, which seats 50,000 people, is usually filled. It is the largest bullfighting ring in the world, and twice as large as any in Spain.

Bullfighting, while often called a sport, is really more of an art form. It is a test of a matador's control over his own fear, the ferocity of the bull, and the expectations of the crowd.

The object of the bullfight is for the matador to kill an untamed bull with a sword. He attempts to do this by following a ritual that has been developed over a very long period of time. The matador is assisted by two mounted *picadors* and three capemen on foot, who are called *banderilleros*.

The fight begins when the ring *presidente* waves his handkerchief and the first bull rushes in. The average bull weighs about 1,100 pounds. Sometimes, dirt is thrown on its back, so that when it runs, the dirt flying off its back will emphasize how quickly it can move.

The bullfight is divided into three parts, called *tercios*. The first *tercio* is called *puyazos*, or stabs. Two *picadors* on horses use lances to weaken the bull's shoulder muscles, causing the head to sag downward. This helps to expose the entry point for the sword's thrust that will end the fight. When the *picadors* leave, the bull is raging but weakened.

The second *tercio* involves the *banderilleros*, who sting the bull with lances and barbed sticks. The bull, bleeding profusely, is furious and begins to charge.

In the final *tercio*, the matador has 16 minutes to kill the bull or the fight is over. He attempts to do this by making daring passes at the bull with his cape, or *muleta*, before thrusting his sword between the animal's shoulder blades into its heart.

The *picadors* lance the bull to weaken and enrage it before its final showdown with the matador.

OTHER SPORTS

Despite the popularity of bullfighting, the biggest spectator sport in Mexico is *fútbol*—which is called soccer in the United States. The new Azteca Stadium in Mexico City seats 100,000, twice as many as the bullring. Games are played during the fall and summer on Sunday afternoons and Thursday evenings.

All along the Pacific coast and in the Southeast, including the Yucatán Peninsula, Mexicans are wild about baseball. They have two major leagues. Children play in school and after-school leagues and Mexican men everywhere are *"sandlot afficionados."*

All forms of sports are practiced in Mexico. Here, people are training in the Japanese martial art of karate.

Jai alai is a handball-like game of Spanish-Basque origin. It is played by either two or four persons on a three-walled court with a hard rubber ball the size of a golfball. A player will hurl the ball against the wall and his opponent will try to catch it in his racket and return it. *Jai alai* is sometimes called *pelota vasca* and Basque Ball.

Cockfighting, which is illegal in the United States, Canada and many other countries, is a popular Mexican sport. These fights take place in an enclosed pit, usually outdoors. Spectators place bets on their favorite gamecocks. At the start of the fight, handlers hold their birds and allow them to peck at each other just out of range. When the birds become angry, they are released and allowed to fight.

Surrounded by oceans on the east and west, Mexicans take every opportunity to go to the beach.

THE CHARROS

Perhaps Mexico's only truly national sport is the *charreria*. It is similar to an American rodeo. The men who participate are called *charros*, and these gentlemen cowboys are considered some of the bravest, strongest men in Mexico.

The skills displayed during a *charreria*—roping, tying, riding or branding cattle—were developed for use in cattle ranching. These skills also made the *charros* excellent cavalrymen in the wars Mexico fought. They would capture the enemy and their cannons by lassoing them as if they were cattle.

A *charreria* or rodeo during a village festival.

After the Mexican Revolution, most large cattle ranches were broken up by the government and the glory days of the *charros* were over. But in order to compete and show off their skills, they developed the *charrerias*. Today, the biggest *charro* rings, called *lienzo charros*, are in Mexico City and Guadalajara. Weekly competitions are held on Sundays.

At the start of the show, the horsemen ride around the ring to salute the judges and the public. The first event, called *cala de caballo*, is meant to demonstrate the rider's control over the horse. The rider guides his horse through a series of difficult maneuvers.

The second event is called the *coleadero*. The *charro* must grab a wild bull by the tail and roll it over on its back. Points are given for how quickly and neatly the *charro* completes this difficult task. The rest of the events involve bronco-bucking, bull-riding and lassoing. Some of these events are the most

exciting of the whole show. Women also compete in their own events at the *charreria*. Even though they ride their horses sidesaddle to preserve their feminity, they are extremely skilled riders.

Charros give much thought to their clothing and often spend a lot of money on their outfits or on equipment for their horses. The typical *charro* dress includes embroidered shirts, *serapes* and dark blue pantaloons embroidered in gold.

Charros are famous ladies' men. They idolize women and can be very romantic. Their strength and bravery make them very attractive to women. They are also very devoted to their horses, and love eating and drinking heartily.

There is an aura of nostalgia about the *charros*, which is a wish to return to a golden past when things were less complicated and people all knew their place.

Besides horsemanship skills, the *charros* must learn how to lasso and rope well.

FESTIVALS

MEXICO CELEBRATES MORE FIESTAS than any other Latin American country. Ever since pre-Spanish times, Mexicans have always believed in the importance and necessity of these celebrations.

The ancient Indian fiestas were mostly somber and religious events. At some of the celebrations, the Indians ate human flesh they had sacrificed to their gods. Today, while some fiestas are solemn affairs, a time to pay homage to a saint, a hero, or a tradition, many others are joyful and full of celebration.

Despite centuries of effort by the colonial Spanish to eradicate pagan rituals and replace them with Christian ones, many of the original pagan holidays are still celebrated. As a result, a fiesta is held somewhere in Mexico almost every day of the year.

Fiestas usually last one or two days, but if the patron saint is especially important, they can last up to a week. The Feria de San Marcos is celebrated in Aguascalientes for ten days every year, starting on St. Mark's Day, which is April 25.

Festivities are usually held around the church and the main plaza, or *zócalo*, both of which are colorfully decorated. During the day, people crowd the open-air markets to buy candy, fruit, toys and local handicrafts. At night, festivities include folk dances, unusual costumes, fireworks and music far into the night. The festivities are usually paid for by someone chosen by the community. It is considered an honor to be chosen. In return for all that money, the fiesta patron receives the gratitude of the people or even a lifetime of prestige.

Above: **Chili-red masks of the devil. Many festivities in Mexico are held to celebrate a religious event.**

Opposite: **Fiestas in Mexico feature ethnic dances, folk music, colorful costumes and happy, smiling faces.**

CALENDAR OF EVENTS

Poet Octavio Paz wrote that Mexico's poverty, "can be measured by the frequency and luxuriousness of our holidays. Wealthy countries have very few: there is neither the time nor the desire for them, and they are not necessary … But how could a poor Mexican live without the two or three annual fiestas that make up for his poverty and misery? Fiestas are our only luxury." Some of the more famous and more important holidays are listed below:

Jan 1	New Year's Day
Feb 5	Constitution Day
Mar 21	Birthday of Benito Juárez
May 1	Labor Day (celebrated with parades)
Sep 16	Independence Day
Nov 20	Anniversary of the Mexican Revolution
Dec 25	Christmas

The following dates are not official national holidays but are widely observed:

Holy Week	prior to Easter
May 5	Anniversary of the Battle of Puebla in 1862
May 10	Mother's Day
Jul 25	Day of St. James
Aug 15	Day of the Virgen de la Asuncion
Aug 25	Day of San Luis
Sep 1	President's annual report to the nation
Oct 12	Dia de la Raza
Nov 2	The Day of the Dead (All Souls Day)
Nov 22	Day of St. Cecilia
Dec 12	Feast of Our Lady of Guadalupe, patron saint of Mexico

The Column of Independence in Mexico City. Once a year, on September 16, Mexico celebrates Independence Day.

INDEPENDENCE DAY

The most important Mexican patriotic fiesta is celebrated on September 16, the anniversary of the day in 1810 when Father Miguel Hidalgo proclaimed Mexico's independence from Spain.

This annual celebration begins on September 15 with a re-enactment of Father Hidalgo's call to battle, called *El Grito de Dolores*. The *El Grito* ceremony takes place simultaneously throughout Mexico at 11 p.m.

In an internationally televised live broadcast, the president of Mexico appears on the central balcony of the National Palace in Mexico City and repeats the 1810 rallying cry of Father Hidalgo. A replica of the bell used to call the battle at the Dolores church is then rung, followed by the ringing of the Metropolitan Cathedral bells.

The *zócalo* below is filled with celebrating Mexicans, in the same

DIA DE LA RAZA

October 12 in the United States is Columbus Day, but in Mexico it is called the Dia de la Raza. Literally translated as "Day of the Race," the Dia de la Raza is meant to commemorate the day the mixture of cultures and races which resulted in Mexico began.

While Americans set aside October 12 as a day to honor the first white man to discover the Americas, the Mexicans attach very little significance to Columbus' discovery. They believe the Americas had already been discovered by their Indian ancestors.

They do, however, consider this day significant in that, after the white man's discovery of their land, Mexico was never the same again.

manner Times Square in New York City is on New Year's Eve. In every municipality in Mexico the same ceremony takes place, with the mayor coming out on the central balcony of City Hall, reciting the *El Grito*, and ringing a replica of the bell of Dolores. In Mexico and the provinces, magnificent fireworks follow.

The *El Grito* is also carried out in the United States in cities with large communities of Mexican-Americans. Top ministers are sent to cities like Los Angeles, San Francisco, San Diego, Chicago and New York City to recite the battle cry and give a speech in Spanish beside city officials.

September 16 is officially Independence Day. Outside Mexico City, bullfights are staged, but the day is usually dedicated to rest. The birth of José Maria Morélos, the hero of the Independence, is celebrated on September 30.

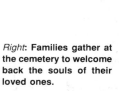

Right: Families gather at the cemetery to welcome back the souls of their loved ones.

Below: Food for the dead is placed on a decorated table that includes a photo of the deceased, along with flowers and other offerings.

THE DAY OF THE DEAD

The Day of the Dead, the most important religious and Indian festival of the year throughout Mexico, is also one of the most peculiar of all Mexican fiestas. It originated in Europe in the 9th century and was introduced into Mexico by the Spaniards after the Conquest. It blended with existing Aztec beliefs concerning death and departed spirits.

For weeks before the occasion, markets and bakeries are filled with special breads baked in human forms; sweets shaped into skulls; toy coffins and papier-mâché skeletons. Flower markets overflow with marigolds, the flower that in Aztec times was sacred to the dead.

On October 31, villagers await the *muertitos chicos*, the souls of dead children. Toy cakes, hot chocolate and honey are left to sweeten their visit to earth. The adult souls are believed to return the following night. Families prepare delicious traditional feasts for their arrival. The dead are believed to eat the spirit of the food.

The next day is the official Day of the Dead. Everyone celebrates by eating the food. Often an all-night candlelight vigil is kept in the town cemetery the night the souls are expected to arrive. Families gather on the graves of their departed to accompany them on their annual journey.

FEAST OF OUR LADY OF GUADALUPE

Every year, on December 12, the day she made her miraculous appearance to the Indian peasant Juan Diego, Mexicans honor the Virgin of Guadalupe. Millions of them make a pilgrimage to the Basilica of the Virgin to thank her for prayers answered. Many crawl up the hill on their hands and knees, painfully bloodying themselves. Despite this, a carnival atmosphere prevails around the church.

Beginning the evening of December 11, the square in front of the Basilica becomes a stage for traditional songs and dances that continue through the night. Because it is close to Christmas, many Christmas activities take place. While the largest celebration is held at the shrine outside Mexico City, many smaller celebrations take place in churches throughout Mexico. Except for the Vatican, the shrine is visited by more people than any other religious site in the Catholic world.

Once every year, a big celebration is held in Guadalupe to honor the Virgin. About six million believers visit the shrine each year.

THE CHRISTMAS SEASON

The Christmas season in Mexico is a combination of Spanish customs left over from the colonial period, and various traditions picked up from the United States.

The *posada* dates from colonial times, when missionaries tried to show the Christmas story for their Indian converts. Literally translated, *posada* means "inn."

Beginning on December 16 and continuing every night through Christmas Eve, *posadas* re-enact Joseph and Mary's search for lodging in Bethlehem. These processions move through the streets carrying lighted candles. At the door of a designated house, the group stops, sings traditional *posada* songs and asks for lodging. After repeated rejections, the door is finally opened. The group joyfully enters and the party begins.

Highlighting the *posada* are traditional food and drink, and for the children, the breaking of the *piñata*. A *piñata* is a clay pot covered with papier-mâché and ribbons and shaped like an animal or a carnival figure.

In most homes, the *piñatas* are filled with candies and toys, although some are filled with money. Blindfolded children take turns swinging a broomstick at the *piñata*, which hangs above them on a rope. When the *piñata* shatters, the children scramble to gather its presents.

While some Mexican families have adopted the American tradition of giving gifts on Christmas Day, Epiphany (January 6), is the traditional gift-giving day in Mexico.

During the Christmas season, the markets are filled with candy, sugared fruits, religious figurines, lanterns, toys, masks, dolls—and *piñatas*.

Epiphany is the day the three gift-bearing kings of the East visited the baby Jesus. Commemorating their arrival in Bethlehem, boys representing the Three Kings wear fake beards, crowns and long robes, and sit in the plazas of towns where children visit them to have their pictures taken.

For parties, a special doughnut-shaped cake is baked with a small doll inside. By tradition, the guest who receives the slice of cake with the doll must give a feast on February 2.

New Year's celebrations in Mexico used to be similar to Thanksgiving celebrations in the United States. They have since become much more like New Year's celebrations in the United States, with lots of parties and celebrating.

Christmas is a time for visiting friends and the exchange of gifts.

FOOD

MEXICO'S CUISINE has been influenced by many countries. Spain—whose cuisine incorporates some Arabic dishes—introduced her new colony to onions, garlic, sugar, beef, pork, chicken and cheese. Catholic nuns were among the first to mix local products with those from Spain, creating truly Mexican cuisine.

French cuisine was introduced during the reign of Maximilian. The crispy-crusted bread commonly associated with France can be found all over Mexico, as well as many kinds of sweet rolls.

Above: **These exotic and fanciful Mexican sweets and desserts taste as good as they look.**

Opposite: **No Mexican meal is complete without tortillas. Tortillas can be found in every restaurant or street stall in Mexico.**

Flan, an egg custard with caramel, is a French dessert that today appears on the menus of almost every Mexican restaurant—both in and out of Mexico.

Other European influences include sausages, honey and beer from Germany, and pasta from Italy. Spices and mangos come aboard ships from the East. American hamburgers, pancakes, pies and doughnuts are becoming more and more popular too.

Many foods taken for granted in the world today originated in Mexico and were introduced to the rest of the world by returning Spanish soldiers in the 16th century.

Corn is probably Mexico's greatest contribution to world cuisine, but the country has also introduced tomatoes, potatoes (both the sweet and the Irish varieties), chocolate, vanilla, various squashes, including pumpkins, peanuts, assorted beans, avocados, chilies, guava, coconuts, pineapples, papayas and turkeys.

STAPLES: CORN TO TORTILLAS

Ancient Mexican cultures introduced two invaluable foods to future generations: corn and chilies. Although many foods are indigenous to ancient Mexico, these two remain unchallenged as the main staples of the Mexican diet.

For thousands of years before Cortés landed in Mexico, corn was the staple of the natives. The Indians called it *toconayo*, which means "our meat." They believed that the gods had molded humans from corn.

The Mexicans, for a time, were known as "the men from corn." All the ancient Indian civilizations devoted ceremonies to their gods and goddesses of corn. Although modern religion does not deify corn, Mexicans continue to revere this ancient source of food. Reverence for

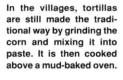

In the villages, tortillas are still made the traditional way by grinding the corn and mixing it into paste. It is then cooked above a mud-baked oven.

CHILIES

Chilies are indigenous to Mexico and play an important part in the country's cuisine.

The Aztecs and Mayans, who cultivated and consumed them, created recipes that are still in use. They believed that chilies were good and had medicinal value, and modern nutritionists agree. A fresh chili is an excellent source of vitamin C and minerals. There are over 100 different types in Mexico, mostly due to the various climates. Each has its own distinct flavor and taste. But generally, the smaller the chili, the hotter it is.

corn can still be observed today: roadworkers clearing brush from the shoulders of the highway rarely cut stalks of wild corn. The same is true of groundskeepers in public parks. As a result, it is not unusual to see corn growing in a downtown plaza or in the middle of a construction site.

No part of the corn plant goes unused: the young, tender ears and husks are used for *tamales* and *atole*; and the corn silk is made into a medicinal tea, said to be good for the kidneys. When it is dried the kernels are used for *masa* (tortilla dough), the husks for *tamales,* and dried stalks for cattle feed. Corn is used in everything from popcorn to cornflakes. It is an ingredient in syrups, desserts, corn starch, oil, grits, coloring for caramel, dextrin, glucose flour, and beer, and as a feed for poultry and livestock.

The most important use of corn is centuries old. Corn forms *masa*, the dough for tortillas and *tamales*. A Mexican table without tortillas is an empty table. Cornmeal tortillas are served with every meal, just as some form of bread or roll is served with most meals in the United States. It is the basis of hundreds of dishes. The first lesson a peasant's daughter learns is how to prepare the *nixtamal* (the corn cooked in a solution of lime and water) for the next day's tortillas.

Moles and *tamales.* The *mole* sauce is a very rich sauce made from more than 30 ingredients, all of which must be ground or puréed. A good *mole* sauce takes two days to prepare.

TRADITIONAL MEALS

Some of Mexico's most well-known and traditional foods are *tacos, enchiladas, tamales* (cornmeal dough filled with meat and chili sauce, wrapped in cornhusks and steamed), *quesadillas* (grilled or fried turnovers with meat, cheese, potatoes, squash blossoms or chili), *chalupas* (tortillas fried and topped with meat and beans, chilies, tomatoes and onions), *gorditas* (small, thick tortillas fried with chopped meat and vegetables, cheese, shredded lettuce, and chili sauce on top), *flautas* (extra-long tacos), and *tostadas*.

Another famous Mexican dish is *chiles rellenos*. Tangy, delicious long green peppers are stuffed with either cheese or ground meat, dipped in egg batter, fried and then simmered in a bland tomato sauce.

For a two-month period beginning in mid-August, there is a special way of serving a dish called *chile en nogada*. The stuffing for this is often made from ground pork, and it is decorated with seeds, sauce and parsley to make the red, white and green colors of the Mexican flag. This dish is also served throughout the country to mark the occasion of the Mexican Independence Day which falls right in the middle of this two-month period (September 16).

Water flavored with a variety of fruit juices are very popular in Mexico. Soft drinks of both Mexican and American types are also a favorite.

TRADITIONAL DRINKS

Mexicans are great coffee drinkers. Coffee is always served at the end of a meal, but never before as most Mexicans would never drink coffee on an empty stomach. Because Mexican coffee is very strong, it is almost always taken with a lot of sugar. A popular coffee is *café con leche*, a blend of strong black coffee and hot milk that's frequently served in a tall, thick glass.

Drinking hot chocolate originated in pre-Columbian times. Today it is a great favorite in Mexico for both breakfast and supper. It is made with a touch of cinnamon, a holdover from the Aztec days when, since there was no sugar, honey and cinnamon were added.

Perhaps not surprisingly, Mexicans drink corn in addition to eating it. *Masa,* the dough used to make tortillas, is the foundation for *atole*, a widely enjoyed beverage prepared by diluting *masa* in water and boiling it until it is as thick as a milkshake.

Mexicans makes a good number of alcoholic beverages from fruits or cactuses. Tequila, *mescal* and *pulque* are all made from the agave plant. Some, such as tequila, are world famous, but others are unappealing to foreigners and are hardly ever seen outside Mexico.

Mexican fast food. Pre-cooked food sold at street side stalls can be served immediately.

MARKETS AND FOOD STALLS

Mexicans shop daily for fresh food at open markets. There are two kinds of markets: temporary and permanent. They are the best places to get fresh fruits and vegetables. Bartering (exchanging one thing for another) is common and even expected in most marketplaces.

Tiendas are small grocery stores that are like the old-fashioned general store. In some of the smaller towns and villages, they also serve as a social center. *Conasupos* are government-owned stores that were originally designed to sell basic staples at controlled prices. In areas too remote to have a permanent store, the government dispatches mobile *conasupos,* usually a large truck or semi-trailer. Prices are usually always lower in *conasupos* than in any other stores.

Finally, there are the *supermercados*, which can be warehouse-size, or simply large *tiendas*. Prices are usually the highest here, but shoppers can choose from a much broader selection of products.

Fondas are eating stalls found in the market that sell meals, including beans, rice, soup and tortillas. Sidewalk stands are another popular source of food.

Even in the cities, the largest meal of the day is lunch, with its place rooted in Mexico's historical observance of the *siesta*.

MEALTIMES

Mexican mornings are long. Breakfast, served between 6 and 8 a.m., usually consists of coffee and bread or pastry, or coffee and *tamales*. Brunch is a heartier meal than breakfast. Eggs, meat or tortillas, accompanied by coffee and milk or fresh-fruit beverages, are served between 11 a.m. and noon.

The Mexican midday meal, *la comida*, is the heaviest and most traditional meal of the day. It is usually not served until around 2 or 3 p.m. The *comida* may include soup, rice or pasta, beans, tortillas or bread, dessert and coffee. The *la comida* may include either beer or fruit juices, but never coffee. After lunch, everything and everybody shuts down for *siesta*.

Between 7 and 8 p.m., Mexicans enjoy their own form of English high tea, called the *merienda*. It consists of a cup of hot chocolate, coffee or *atole*, and some pastries and *tamales*. *Cena*, or supper, is the third major meal of the day. It can be served anytime between 7.30 p.m. and midnight, but is usually eaten between 9 and 10 p.m. It is lighter than the *la comida* and might include leftovers from lunch, such as tacos, or tortillas.

THE MEXICAN KITCHEN

UTENSILS

While many Mexican kitchens have modern utensils and appliances like blenders and food processors, many of their cooking tools have been around for thousands of years. Mexican cooks rely extensively on clay cookware, bowls and pitchers. The following are some of the more traditional Mexican cooking tools:

Bean Masher: Usually made of wood.
Molinillo: Chocolate beater. Usually made of beautifully carved wood.
Comal: A round, flat plate of tin or unglazed earthenware on which tortillas are cooked.
Flan Mold: A three-piece tin utensil for cooking flan in a water bath in the oven.

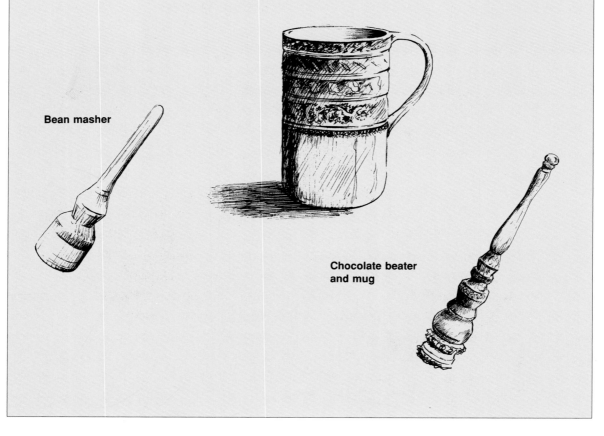

Bean masher

Chocolate beater
and mug

Metate: A sloping, rectangular piece of volcanic rock supported on three stout legs. Together with a *metlapil* (stone rolling pin), it is used for grinding corn, chilies, *cacao* and other ingredients for making sauces.

Molcajete and Tejolate: Mortar made from porous, volcanic stone and pestle. Used for grinding spices and making sauces. Considered indispensable in many Mexican kitchens.

Chiquihuite: The traditional tortilla basket made of woven reed grass and lined with a cloth that covers the tortillas to keep them warm.

Tortilla Press: Used for rolling and shaping tortillas.

TECHNIQUES

Cooking Mexican food requires no frighteningly precise techniques, like those of French cuisine, for example. It only requires a great deal of preparation and cutting.

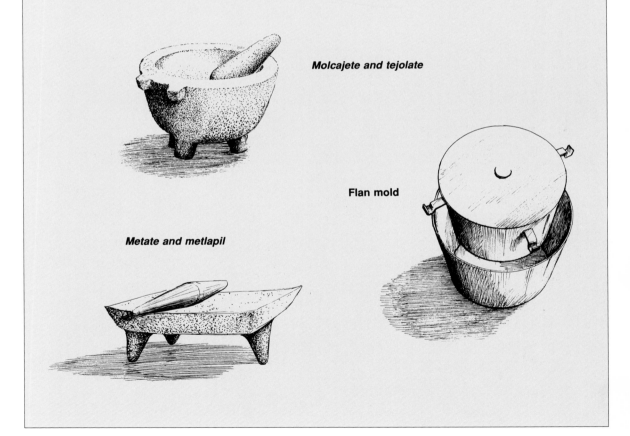

Molcajete and tejolate

Flan mold

Metate and metlapil

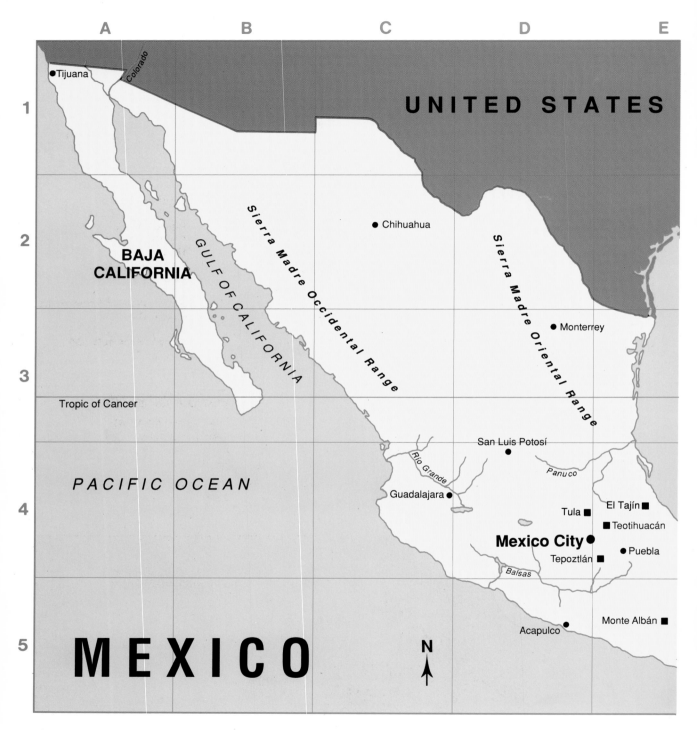

A B C D E

1

UNITED STATES

●Tijuana

Colorado

2

BAJA
CALIFORNIA

●Chihuahua

GULF OF CALIFORNIA

Sierra Madre Occidental Range

Sierra Madre Oriental Range

●Monterrey

3

Tropic of Cancer

San Luis Potosí ●

PACIFIC OCEAN

Rio Grande

Panuco

Guadalajara ●

4

Tula ■   El Tajín ■

■ Teotihuacán

Mexico City ●

Tepoztlán ■   ● Puebla

Balsas

5

MEXICO

N
↑

Acapulco ●

Monte Albán ■

124

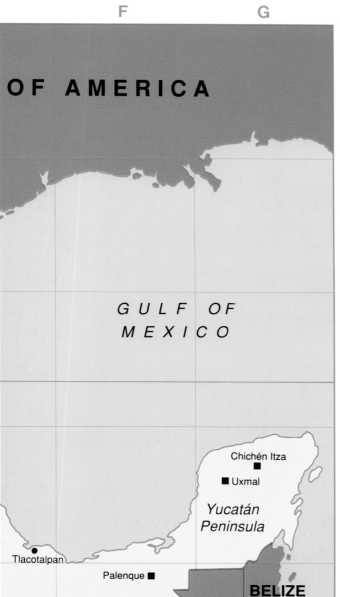

F　　　G

OF AMERICA

*GULF OF
MEXICO*

Chichén Itza ■

■ Uxmal

*Yucatán
Peninsula*

● Tlacotalpan

Palenque ■

BELIZE

● Tehuantepec

GUATEMALA

HONDURAS

Acapulco   D5

Baja California   A2
Balsas   D4
Belize   G5

Chichén Itza   G4
Chihuahua   C2
Colorado River A1

El Tajín   E4

Guadalajara   C4
Guatemala   G5
Gulf of California   B2
Gulf of Mexico   F3

Honduras   G5

Mexico City   D4
Monte Albán   E5
Monterrey   D3

Pacific Ocean   A4

Palenque   F5
Panuco   D4
Puebla   E4

Río Grande   C4

San Luis Potosí   D4
Sierra Madre Occidental
    Range   B2
Sierra Madre Oriental
    Range   D2

Tehuantepec   E5
Teotihuacán   E4
Tepoztlán   E4
Tlacotalpan   E4
Tijuana   A1
Tropic of Cancer   A3
Tula   D4

United States of America   C1
Uxmal   G4

Yucatán Peninsula   G4

─────── International Boundary
─────── Tropic of Cancer
● Capital
● City
■ Ancient site
〜〜 River

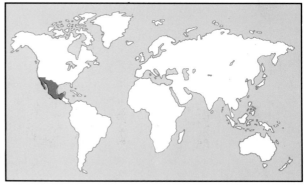

125

QUICK NOTES

LAND AREA
767,919 square miles

POPULATION
89 million (estimated)

CAPITAL
Mexico City

STATES
Aguascalientes, Baja California Norte, Baja California Sur, Campeche, Chiapas, Chihuahua, Coahuila, Colima, Durango, Guanajuato, Guerrero, Hidalgo, Jalisco, Mexico, Michoacán, Morelos, Nayarit, Nuevo León, Oaxaca, Puebla, Querétaro, Quintana Roo, San Luis Potosí, Sinaloa, Sonora, Tabasco, Tamaulipas, Tlaxcala, Veracruz, Yucatán, Zacatecas

IMPORTANT CITIES AND TOWNS
Aguascalientes, Acapulco, Ciudad Juaréz, Chihuahua, Cuernavaca, Culiacán, Durango, Ensenada, Guadalaraja, Irapuato, Jalapa, León, Los Mexicali, Mochis, Monterrey, Morelia, Mérida, Mazatlan, Nuevo Laredo, Poza Rica, Pueblo, San Luis Potosí, Tampico, Tapachula, Toluca, Tapachula, Torreón, Veracruz

ANCIENT RUINS AND ARCHEOLOGICAL SITES
Mayan Palace— Palenque (Mayan)
  Temple of the Inscriptions
Olmec Pit—Tabasco (Olmec)
Pyramid of the Magician—Uxmal (Mayan)
  "The Nunnery"
Pyramid of the Niches—El Tajín (Huastecs)

Pyramid of the Sun—Teotihuacán (unknown)
  Pyramid of the Moon
"The Dancers"—Monte Albán (Oaxaca)
Temple of the Rising Star—Tula (Toltec)
Temple of the Warriors—Chichén Itza (Mayan)
  Toltec Ballcourt
  El Castillo Pyramid

HIGHEST POINT
Orizaba, also called Citlaltpétl (18,696 feet)

NATIONAL LANGUAGE
Spanish

MAJOR RELIGION
Roman Catholic

CURRENCY
Peso (1 peso equals 100 centavos)

MAIN EXPORTS
Petroleum and petroleum products, silver, copper, zinc, sulfur, salt, coffee, cotton, fruits, vegetables, shrimp

IMPORTANT ANNIVERSARIES
Independence Days (Sept 15 and 16)
Guadalupe Day (Dec 2)

POLITICAL LEADERS
Miguel Hidalgo y Costillo—revolutionary leader
Benito Juárez—national hero, President of Mexico in 1857–65 and 1867–72
Porfirio Díaz—dictator of Mexico (1876–1911)
Francisco I. Madero—revolutionary leader, former President of Mexico (1911–13)

GLOSSARY

atole	A popular drink made from corn.
adobe	Sun-dried brick.
Creoles	Spaniards born in Mexico.
ejidos	Communal farmlands.
mestizo	Person of mixed European and Indian ancestry.
peninsulars	Spaniards born in Spain but living in Mexico, usually representing the Spanish crown.
serape	A colorful blanket.
zócalo	A central plaza or square around which villages and cities are organized. The *zócalo* is the center of the town's activities. The main plaza in Mexico City is simply called the Zócalo.

BIBLIOGRAPHY

Casagrande, Louis B and Johnson, S.A.: *Focus on Mexico: Modern Life in an Ancient Land*, Lerner 1986.

Hall, Barbara J.: *Mexico in Pictures*, Sterling Publishing Company 1986.

Lewis, Oscar.: *The Children of Sanchez*, Vintage 1961.

Muller, Kal and Garcia-Oropeza, Guillermo.: *Insight Guides: Mexico*, Prentice–Hall Travel, 1989.

Oster, Patrick.: *The Mexicans: A Personal Portrait of a People*, William Morrow and Company, 1989.

Riding, Alan.: *Distant Neighbours: A Portrait of the Mexicans*, Vintage Books, 1986.

INDEX

Acapulco 11, 43, 97
Agustín de Iturbe, Emperor 23
Aztecs 19, 58, 76, 84, 92

bullfight 98

cannibalism 45, 105
Carranza, Venustiano 26
Catholic 70, 72
chilies 117, 118
cockfight 101
coffee 119
Columbus 109
constitution 26, 29, 70
corn 38, 115, 116
Cortés, Hernán 21, 79
cotton 39

David Siqueros 86, 87
Day of the Dead 58, 110
debt 35
desert 8, 13
Díaz, Porfirio 25, 94
diseases 64

English 75, 77
executive branch 30

fiesta 105

grey whale 15

hat dance 93
Hidalgo y Costillo 23, 108
holiday 106, 107
housing 64, 66
Huichols 49, 56

Ice Age 46
Indian 47, 76

José Orozco 86, 87
Juan Diego 71, 111
Juárez, Benito 23, 24, 70
judicial system 30

junior 78

legislative branch 30
literacy 65

machismo 58
Madero, Francisco 25, 26
malinchismo 79
mariachis 91
Maximilian, Emperor 24,
Mayan 10, 18, 84, 76, 92
Mesoamerica 7, 19, 46
mestizo 45, 48
Mexico City 67
missionaries 22
Moctezuma 21
Monte Albán 11, 17

Olmecs 17, 46, 84

Paz, Octavio 95, 106
petroleum 35, 40, 41
piñata 112
plaza 53, 105
political parties 32
pollution 67
poncho 50
Pope John Paul II 72
population 7, 49
posada 112
pottery 88
pyramid 84

Quetzalcóatl 20, 21

rains 13
Rivera, Diego 19, 21, 23, 86, 87
rodeo 102

Santa Anna, de Antonio Lopez 23
siesta 63
silver 40
soccer 100
sombrero 50
Sundays 97

tamales 117, 118
Tenochtitlán 19, 84
Teotihuacán 20
tequila 119
time 62
tortillas 116
transportation 42
Tropic of Cancer 12

United States 7, 23, 24, 33, 41
utensils 122

Villa, Pancho 26
Virgin of Guadalupe 71, 111
volcanoes 9, 11
volodores 93

War of Independence 70
War of Reform 24
weaving 88

Zapata, Emiliano 26
zócalo 105, 108

Picture Credits

Victor Englebert, Marcelo Montecino, South American Pictures (Kimball Morrison, Tony Morrison), Liba Taylor.